The Bougainvillea Growers Handbook for New Zealanders

Jan Iredell

David Bateman

First published in 1989 by
David Bateman Ltd
'Golden Heights', 32-34 View Road, Glenfield, Auckland, New Zealand

ISBN 0 908610 99 8

Typeset by Visual Solutions Ltd, Auckland
Printed in Singapore
Jacket design by Mick Brabant

The Bougainvillea Growers Handbook for New Zealanders

Contents

ACKNOWLEDGEMENTS

I would like to express my gratitude to the people who have assisted me with information during the researching of this book: the Killie Campbell Africana Library, University of Natal, Republic of South Africa for material on the bougainvilleas grown by William Poulton; Royal Horticultural Society, London, for the RHS Colour Chart which is invaluable in identifying the colour of flowers; Jimmy Dyce, Loughton, Essex for expediting a copy of the RHS Chart in short order; Dr R.E. Holttum, Richmond, Surrey for sending me copies of his notes on bougainvilleas; Madame Ohn Sett of the Singapore Botanic Gardens; Professor J.V. Pancho, Institute of Biological Sciences, University of the Philippines, for information on cultivars; Dr S.C. Sharma, National Botanical Research Institute, Lucknow, India for copies of work done on Bougainvilleas; Dr B. Singh, Indian Agricultural Research Institute, New Delhi, India.

I am especially grateful to Professor Colin Dobson, University of Queensland, Australia for his assistance in editing the final draft.

Special thanks to Evan William, Alstoneville, NSW, Australia; Bill Starke, Castle Hill Nurseries, Sydney, Australia; Philip Wood, Perth, Western Australia; Dennis Hearn, Tropicus Nursery, Darwin, Australia.

I would also like to thank the follow people for their help: Cedric Bond, Sydney, Australia; Alan Branch, Wallsend, Australia; Ed Fraser, Brisbane, Australia; the late David Lemmer, Harare, Zimbabwe; Meg Lloyd, Brisbane, Australia; Gerald Schofield and Dunrobin Nursery, Natal, Republic of South Africa; Ali Lloyd, Brisbane, Australia; Mr Ken Stevenson, Prosperine, Australia; Mr George Trapnell, Brisbane, Australia; Tim Willing, Broome, Western Australia; Nick Wolverson, Brisbane, Australia.

I owe a very deep debt of gratitude to my family, especially

Peter for the photography, and his patience and support throughout the project, without which it would not have been possible; to Jon who has been especially helpful with the chapter on genetics and to Penny for whom the bougainvillea cultivar Penelope is named.

Last but not least thank you to my friend, Ros Munro, who typed up that very first draft.

I thank you all.

AUTHOR'S NOTE

Due to the great demand for a book on the growing of bougainvilleas it was decided to publish this pocket guide pending the publication of a definitive study.

The following book will be bigger and more detailed and will cover every aspect of bougainvilleas and their cultivation. This major work has come about following 10 years of research and over 14 years experience plus many thousands of miles of travel to check, photograph and compare the cultivars. There will be detailed descriptions and photographs of each cultivar, showing the distinctive differences between them, and the names by which each is known. This then will be a guide to standardisation of cultivar names and an aid to the correction of incorrectly named cultivars.

Although bougainvilleas are the most popular and most widely grown tropical vines, there are no active bougainvillea societies other than the one in India, the address of which is:

The Bougainvillea Society of India
Division of Floriculture and Landscaping
Indian Agricultural Research Institute
New Delhi 110 012
INDIA

This is probably because there has been no means of reference for accurate identification of cultivars. A definitive work on bougainvilleas, which is intended to follow the publication of this book, will provide that reference.

Any persons interested in forming a bougainvillea society should contact the author c/o the publisher.

PREFACE

Most of the bougainvillea cultivars have many synonyms, which confuse both growers and collectors alike. Listed are more than 100 cultivars with general descriptions and photographs of representative varieties.

As an illustration, the original hybrid B. X buttiana was distributed around the world as 'Mrs. Butt', but in the USA it was called 'Crimson Lake' for the colour. In later years, other varieties occurred and were imported into various countries from different sources and we now have many names for the same cultivars. Indeed, newly imported cultivars are often given catchy marketing names without thought to their original identity, thereby adding to the confusion.

I hope my book will be of use to all who love bougainvilleas and wish to grow them well.

NOTE ON CULTIVAR NAMES

The Index of Cultivar Names (p.92) provides a quick guide to alternative names for each variety, which in some cases are numerous and can be confusing. These names are listed alphabetically with the synonyms alongside.

Chapter One

INTRODUCTION & HISTORY

Bougainvilleas are beautiful climbing plants indigenous to tropical South America. They are adaptable, long flowering and can take many forms, from the disciplined Bonsai, through potted plants of varying sizes, to small flowering trees (standards), espalier, clipped hedges, lawn specimens, or a tangle of riotous colour, when a group of one or more varieties are planted together.

Bougainvilleas climb by sending out strong canes armed with stiff, curved thorns. In nature this helps them to penetrate undergrowth and trees to reach the light where they fan out and flower prolifically.

Bougainvilleas respond well to pruning (the long canes are easily removed with sharp secateurs) and will grow into vivid, long-flowering, shrubby plants for sunny situations. They are relatively free of pests and disease, and will tolerate rather harsh soil conditions. I have seen bougainvilleas growing well in shallow pots of gravelly soil and in stony ground where there is no apparent topsoil, but they do best in sandy soils and volcanic loam. Growth is slower in stony ground and the plant is more compact with shorter internodes. They can be grown up to 3000m, and can be seen growing well at this altitude in Addis Ababa, Ethiopia.

Bougainvilleas will come up trumps and reward you with a wonderful display of exotic blooms for months on end, but all cultivars need *plenty of sunshine*; the more the better. Bougainvilleas fade and look 'sad' when they are grown in the shade.

Bougainvilleas come in any number of colours, from white through palest pink to deep magenta; from pale gold through orange and scarlet, and from the palest of iridescent lavender to deep rich purple. Many varieties change colour between the immature bud stage and mature bract stage, thereby giving very subtle and varied colour effects; some have several different colours on the one plant. The only colour not represented is true blue.

There are many ways of growing bougainvilleas, and no matter how small your growing space, you will be well rewarded if you include at least one among your collection of plants. Many varieties do not grow large and are admirably suited to small gardens or to pots for the balcony.

Bougainvilleas are generally regarded as not being especially attractive to birdlife; however, there is lively interaction within a patch of bougainvilleas which provides a habitat for many species of birds, a food source with nectar and insects, nesting sites and shelter from predators.

In Australia, mistletoe birds, honeyeaters and willie wagtails nest in bougainvilleas, whilst superb starlings and silvereyes flit in and out seeking insects. In Africa, Hunter's sunbirds nest in bougainvilleas and the thickets are frequented by superb and Hildebrandt's starlings, finches (including the purple Grenadier and Cordon Bleu); members of the thrush family, and paradise flycatchers.

In America, red cardinals, goldfinches, mockingbirds and

larks regularly use bougainvilleas as habitat. In New Zealand, warblers, fantails, hedge sparrows and silvereyes find the bougainvillea environment a source of food and shelter.

The flowers themselves in many places are also attended by tiny flower spiders which stand poised to pounce on any unsuspecting insect.

Nectar-feeding butterflies and moths, such as monarchs, white cabbage butterflies, skippers, hawk moths and swallowtails, are attracted to the nectaries of bougainvillea flowers. None of these creatures feed on the plant in their larval stages, so they are not pests.

A BRIEF HISTORY

Most gardeners are familiar with bougainvilleas, and the many specimens for the garden are the result of much interbreeding between three species, although there are at least 18 species described from South America.

This wonderful climbing shrub was discovered by the French botanist Philibert Commerson, who saw and described it in Rio de Janeiro. Commerson was the botanist on the French ship *Bordeuse,* which sailed around the world between 1766 and 1769 under the command of Louis Antoine de Bougainville, for whom the genus is named. Bougainville voyaged to discover new territories in the Pacific for France, after that country had lost its Canadian empire.

The generic name was initially published as *Buginvillea* in A.L. de Jusseau's *Genera Plantarium* in 1789, 20 years after Commerson found the plant in Brazil. The name was subsequently spelled a number of different ways until it was finally corrected to *Bougainvillea* and published in the *Index Kewensis* (Suppl. 9, 1931–35)

Willdenow originally described *Bougainvillea spectabilis* in Linnaeus' *Species Plantarium* from dried specimens collected in Brazil, but did not detail how it grew and there was little to differentiate *B. spectabilis* from *B. glabra*. The original description of *B. glabra* was made by Choisy in 1849 from dried specimens collected from a number of places in South America. Choisy and Heimerl recognised *B. glabra* as a distinct species and redescribed *B. spectabilis*, which was then distinguished from the hairless or nearly hairless *B. glabra* by its hairy leaves, canes, bracts and flower tubes. *B. spectabilis* flowers in response to a cool, dry season, whereas *B. glabra* will flower continuously and profusely in the tropics.

HISTORY OF CULTIVATION

Bougainvillea spectabilis was the first species introduced to horticulture in Europe, and was grown and flowered successfully in greenhouses in both Europe and England in the early 1800s. *Bougainvillea glabra* was introduced some years later. About this time other specimens of *Bougainvillea glabra* and *Bougainvillea spectabilis* which had differences in colour and size of bract were introduced.

Nurseries in France and England which specialised in growing tropical plants provided specimens which were subsequently grown in Australia and many other places. Kew Gardens distributed many plants to British colonies throughout the tropics and subtropics.

The discovery, by Mrs R.V. Butt of Trinidad, of a crimson-bracted bougainvillea in a priest's garden in Cartagena is a major event in the history of bougainvilleas. This plant was thought to be a distinct species because it had different habits and appearance and it was named

Bougainvillea buttiana for the lady who found it. However, it was subsequently found to be a natural hybrid — *B.* X *buttiana* (X signifies hybrid origin.)

Bougainvillea X *buttiana* was easy to propagate from cuttings collected in Trinidad, where it was widely distributed. This lovely plant is still a favourite and is still known as Mrs Butt's bougainvillea to this day.

Bougainvillea 'Mrs Butt' was introduced into America by the Reasoner brothers of Florida in 1913, and they sold it as 'Crimson Lake' because the bracts had such startling colour. Plants sent to Kew Gardens were raised as stock to send in 1923 to New Zealand, India, Australia, East Africa and other British Colonies.

Professor S.C. Harland proved that *Bougainvillea* X *buttiana* was a hybrid when he crossed a variety of *B. glabra* with a 'local pink bougainvillea' in Peru (almost certainly *B. peruviana* which did not appear in cultivation until the early 1900s, when Mr R.O. Williams reported it as a new pink bougainvillea which had been introduced to Trinidad from Ecuador). It seems likely that many other hybrid crosses have occurred naturally. During the 1930s when *Bougainvillea spectabilis, B. glabra* and *B. peruviana* were grown together, hybrid seedlings began to appear spontaneously in East Africa, India, the Canary Islands, Australia, America, and the Philippines.

Most seed collected was of unknown pollen parentage and many plants now exist which are intermediate between *Bougainvillea glabra* and *B. spectabilis*. Chance seedlings grown from either *B. spectabilis* or *B. glabra,* or seed collected from one plant, show a large range in colour and size of bract, and considerable variation in the degree of furriness on the leaves and the number of thorns.

Chapter Two

THE SPECIES AND HYBRIDS

The species

Bougainvilleas produce massive displays of flowers of unsurpassed brilliance, in an enormous range of colours in even the toughest conditions.

They are plastic in form and can be grown into any conceivable shape. They are hardy, forgiving, and relatively free of pests and disease.

The genus *Bougainvillea* has only three among eighteen recognised species represented in horticulture. These are *Bougainvillea spectabilis, Bougainvillea glabra, Bougainvillea peruviana.*

Three major hybrid groups are also recognised, namely: *B.*X *buttiana* (*glabra* X *peruviana*), *B.*X *spectoperuviana* (*spectabilis* X *peruviana*), and *B.*X *spectoglabra* (*spectabilis* X *glabra*).

Bougainvilleas in gardens today come from both natural and fostered hybrids and many are from some spontaneous changes (bud-sports; branches with different coloured bracts to the parent) among existing types.

Many of the hybrids from *B. peruviana* have given rise to either bud-sports or mutations. Others have produced branches either with double bracts or with variegated leaves, which has added further dimensions to the variety of cultivars of *Bougainvillea*.

Bougainvillea spectabilis: was the first species of bougainvillea collected and was described from dried specimens by Willdenow (1798). It is a large climbing shrub with stout thorns, hairy stems and foliage and pale corky bark. It has an impressive seasonal display of flowers.

Thorns — woody, strong, hairy and somewhat curved.

Leaves — large, ovate to rounded, somewhat wavy along the margin, leathery in texture, and hairy underneath.

Branching — close and short, giving rise to a very dense plant. Inflorescences multiple and terminal in the axillary branches.

Flowering — either during dry season or in response to cool dry weather.

Bracts — large, ovate, obtuse at tip, quilted in appearance, and coloured rose, rusty red and purple.

Flowers — cream in colour,slender, very hairy tubes with fine ribs and a narrow mouth. The tube is only slightly swollen at the base.

Bougainvillea glabra: is a climbing evergreen shrub with spreading, spiny branches originally named and described by Choisy (1849).

Thorns — short, thin and curved at the tips.

Leaves — fairly evenly elliptical, widest about the middle. Puberulent.

Branching — close with short inflorescences of flowers all along the canes.

Flowering — either continuous or nearly so.

Bracts — pointed and triangular which vary in size, shape, and colour, but only in white and shades of mauve and purple.

Flowers — conspicuous; tubular, swollen at the base; short hairs to 1mm. Corolla white to cream in colour.

***Bougainvillea peruviana*:** a climbing, spiny, spreading shrub with greenish bark. It has similar habits to *B.* X *buttiana* but it is less robust. *B. peruviana* was named and described by Humboldt and Bonpland (1808).

Spines — thin, straight in youth, and curved when older.

Leaves — thin, quite glabrous, ovate to broadly ovate, acute at tip and cuneate at base; petioles long, slender, hairless.

Branching — loose and open; terminal inflorescences.

Flowering — recurrent after strong vegetative growth in response to dry weather.

Bracts — small, rounded, delicate and crinkled, pale magenta to pink in colour.

Flowers — tubular and very slender, quite smooth apart from a few hairs on the bracts, yellowish colour. Stamens shorter than the perianth.

***Bougainvillea X buttiana*:** a hybrid, is a large woody climber with open branches, large dark green leaves and stout straight thorns. It has habits similar to *B. peruviana,* but is more vigorous in growth, and exhibits the minimal hairiness (puberulence) of *B. glabra* with bract and flower traits intermediate between both parent species. The hybrid was described and named by Holttum and Standley (1947).

Thorns — strong, short and straight, rather flattened at base.

Leaves — very large on main stems, either broadly ovate or slightly heart shaped, apex narrows abruptly to a narrow triangular tip, upper surface dark, dull green with paler veins, very short copious straight hairs on both surfaces.

Branching — loose and open.

Flowering — crowded inflorescences first appear at the end of branches and then along canes. Free flowering, with flushes of flower all year.

Bracts — rounded, cordate base, rounded tip, colours from white tinged with pink, through yellow-orange, pink to deep crimson.

Flowers — conspicuous in some cultivars, incomplete in others. Complete flowers are tubular, gently swollen in lower half, either cream or tinged with pink. The tube often has a colour close to that of the bract.

The hybrids

Cytogenetic studies have been done in India (Zadoo *et al.* 1975) on the bougainvillea hybrids and they have been classified in three distinct groups:

B.X buttiana	(*glabra* X *peruviana*)
B.X spectoperuviana	(*spectabilis* X *peruviana*)
B.X spectoglabra	(*spectabilis* X *glabra*)

The *buttiana* group, represented by the original hybrid *Bougainvillea* X *buttiana* 'Mrs Butt' and a number of its bud-sports are all morphologically similar.

B.X spectoperuviana, represented by the original hybrid 'Mrs H.C. Buck' and its hybrids are also morphologically similar. There are other known *spectoperuviana* hybrids and it is hoped that descriptions and comparisons can be done later.

In the group *B.X spectoglabra,* 'Sanderiana' is a known representative cultivar in Australia.

Another group of cultivars, some of which have distinctive appearance, are of undetermined parentage. Perhaps they are recombinations with *B. peruviana*, characters of *B. peruviana* being apparent.

The cultivars need to be cross-checked at their source of origin and from there assessment regarding their hybrid ancestry may be considered.

CLASSIFICATION OF PLANT NAMES

Plants within a species which show minor differences from each other are called 'cultivars'. These differences sometimes occur between seedlings and sometimes as a mutation or 'bud-sport'; the plant is usually identified and named by its originator. *The International Code of Nomenclature for Cultivated Plants* covers the special categories and names of cultivated plants.

The word 'cultivar' is a contraction of the phrase 'cultivated variety' and is synonymous with the word 'variety'. A cultivar should be distinguished from a 'botanical variety' which occurs naturally. The cultivar should have a proper name which propagators can recognise and which cannot be confused with the names of other cultivars.

Multiple names for the single cultivar can arise by accident and sometimes they are added deliberately; in any event it creates confusion. The principle about the names of cultivars is that the first name given has priority and should not be changed unless that name is occupied by another cultivar.

The scientific name of plants includes a name for the genus, the species, and, when the plant has horticultural varieties, the cultivar.

For example:	genus	-	*Bougainvillea*
	species	-	*glabra*
	cultivar	-	'Easter Parade'

This can be written either:

— with the abbreviation cv. preceding the cultivar name e.g. *Bougainvillea glabra* cv. Easter Parade;
— with quotation marks e.g. *Bougainvillea glabra* 'Easter Parade';
— or, when the species is not known, *Bougainvillea* 'Easter Parade'.

If from a major hybrid group, then the name may be written X. *buttiana* (X signifying hybrid origin), e.g. *B*.X *buttiana* 'Mrs Butt'; *B*.X *spectoglabra* 'Sanderiana'.

ENVIRONMENTAL COLOUR CHANGES

The bracts can change colour in different environments, which often makes the identity of cultivars confusing. Plants grown in full sunshine and low humidity have bracts with more intense colour than plants grown in humid tropical conditions and in glasshouses.

The magenta colouring of the bracts consists of bands of betacyanins (red-purple pigments) and betaxanthins (yellow-orange pigments). Light intensity influences the deposition of these pigments; betacyanins are the most responsive. Thus a rich magenta-red bougainvillea grown in full, clear sunlight will be more coppery in colour than plants grown in a glasshouse or humid tropical conditions. Purple cultivars grown in the same intense conditions can become quite mauve in colour.

The light is more diffuse in humid hot climates than in dry air. Plants grown indoors are paler as are those grown in the shade because they get less light and deposit less pigment in their bracts. It is interesting that the white, gold, orange and red bracts of *B.*X *buttiana* cultivars all show a tendency to become purple as they fade. This appears as tinges of purple at the tips and edges of bracts, particularly in those exposed to the maximum amount of light. *B. spectabilis* has bracts which change to a more coppery tone as they fade. The bracts on *B. glabra* varieties change little but can produce more red tonings when they fade.

DOUBLE-BRACTED CULTIVARS

Double-bracted bougainvilleas have evolved by mutation (bud-sports) from the cultivars of the *B.*X *buttiana* (*glabra* X *peruviana*) group. They have no flowers due to the doubling, having 20 to 40 small bracts to a cyme instead of the usual three. This results in densely packed heads of 'flowers' (bracts) and there are five distinct colours.

Most have sported branches with variegated leaves, thereby increasing the number of variations within the double-bracted group to nine. These are:

Mahara Double Red — double red
syn. Manila Magic Red
syn. Klong Fire
syn. Carmerita

Cinderella — double red with variegated leaves

Mahara Orange — double orange
syn. Roseville's Delight — also with variegated foliage
syn. Doubloon
syn. Thai Gold

Mahara Pink — double pink
syn. Los Banos Beauty — also with variegated foliage
syn Pagoda Pink
syn. Pink Champagne

Mahara Off-White — double white with pink-tipped bracts
syn. Bridal Bouquet
syn. Cherry Blossom
syn. Limberlost Beauty
syn. Eastern White
syn. Thai Queen

Coconut Ice — variegated-leafed form of above
syn. Margarita

Double Yellow — double bright yellow

VARIEGATED CULTIVARS

Variegated bud-sports have occurred in many of the hybrid bougainvilleas, adding yet another dimension to the range available. Some of these have been imported and given different names for marketing; others have occurred spontaneously.

Many of these have independent names, whereas others have not yet been named.

Known variegated cultivars are:

Name	Origin
Cinderella	(Klong Fire)
Coconut Ice	(Limberlost Beauty)
Freckleface	(Mrs McClean)
Golden Summers	(Penelope)
Harlequin	(Mary Palmer)
Harrissii	(Sanderiana)
Mistress Columbine	(Mrs Butt)
Orange Picot	(Rosenka)
Phoenix	(Mrs Butt)
Raspberry Ice	(Reported as Mrs Butt)
Scarlet Pimpernel	(Scarlet O'Hara)
Scarlet Queen Variegata	(Scarlet Queen)

Other cultivars have produced variegated forms but they as yet have not been independently named. They are:

Blondie
Lady Mary Baring
Pagoda Pink
Texas Dawn
Thai Gold
Tango
Temple Fire

BI-COLOURED CULTIVARS

Bougainvillea X *specto-peruviana* has given rise to a particularly beautiful bi-coloured cultivar. It has both deep pink and white bracts intermingled in a cyme and on different branches giving a wonderful effect. The bracts are very large, are produced in profusion and in recurring flushes throughout the year. Originally named 'Mary Palmer' for the lady in whose garden it first grew, it has been marketed under different names in different countries. This plant has also given rise to a variegated-leafed form with the same bi-coloured bracts, which is a particularly bright and attractive cultivar.

Chapter Three

THE CULTIVARS A TO Z

African Sunset: *spectabilis*, not vigorous, bracts changing from pink through salmon orange finally to red.

Alba: syn. Snow White. Pure white bracts, reflexed and pointed. Leaves are long, narrow and pointed, growth in young plants spindly, responding well to regular pruning. Has several flushes of flowers each year.

Alex Butchart: *spectabilis* cultivar; vigorous grower, leaves somewhat furry to touch, bracts long and oval, with prominent green veining. Somewhat quilted in appearance and rich rosy red in colour. Seasonal flowering habit.

Alison Davey: leaves large, flat, mid-green, smooth and pointed. New growth bronze; habit is moderate to large. Makes a spectacular show with very large flowering heads of bracts opening coppery red and finally iridescent magenta. Recurring flowering habit. Thorns medium and straight.

Apple Blossom: syn. Audrey Grey, Jamaica White. Medium grower of the *buttiana* group. Leaves are rounded, large, dark green and smooth; thorns medium, bracts medium size, white with flush of pink. Very pretty but rather shy flowering.

Asia: medium grower; very good for pots and banks as tends to be rather flat in growth habit. Leaves oval with pointed tips and frequently have distortions with silvery-grey markings. Bracts medium size, oval; sometimes have distortions as in the leaves. Brilliant magenta red-purple. Flowers all along the canes. Several flushes of flowers a year. Thorns slender and straight.

Badgen's Beauty: rampant grower with large, dark green, glossy leaves; large rich purple bracts in profusion. Thorns large and curved. Can be grown in confined spaces but needs firm control.

Barbara Karst: syn. Crimson Jewel. Moderate grower; bracts red and flower all along the canes; several flushes of flowers in a year. Leaves dull, dark green, broadly ovate with pointed tips. Thorns medium and straight.

Beaujolais: rather low-growing and spreading in habit; leaves medium green and rather dull in appearance. Bracts large, colour of port wine and tend to be seasonal in habit. Excellent for banks or ground cover. Thorns medium and straight.

Beryl's Red: leaves mid to dark green, broadly ovate, smooth, margins wavy, tip pointed. Bracts medium size, thin-textured, slightly coppery red on opening but overall effect is light red. Habit is slightly drooping and thorns are medium and slightly curved.

Betty Lavers: medium grower, bracts gold through to mauve pink.

B.J.F. Bailey: *spectabilis* variety with furry leaves, large thorns and vigorous habit. Bracts are medium size, oval and blood red in colour.

Blondie: syn. Hugh Evans, Fair Lady. Delicate, medium grower; leaves light green, narrow and quite distinctive in appearance. Young leaf growth coppery. Thorns medium and straight. Bracts medium, thin in texture, nearly elliptic in shape; pale gold-orange on opening and fading to very soft pink. Responds very well to pruning and a good variety for pot or standard. Does not like prolonged wet weather, and sheds its leaves.

Bois-de-Rose: beautiful, dusty pink *spectabilis* with furry leaves and vigorous growth; seasonal flowering. Thorns large and slightly recurved.

Brilliance: medium grower with lax pendulous habit; leaves ovate, tapering at each end. Petiole is quite long, dark green in colour. Bracts ovate with pointed end and brilliant fiery red. Recurring flushes of flowers. Thorns long and slender.

Camarillo Fiesta: leaves dark green, large, dull and markedly rounded. Habit rather leggy but flowers so brilliant it is worth keeping it pruned. Bracts very large, round and open; a burnt orange fading to a coppery iridescent red. Thorns medium and stout. Seasonal in flower habit but can be induced to flower more in dry conditions.

Carnarvon: similar to many other *spectabilis* cultivars; vigorous, furry leaves, large stout thorns and seasonal flowering habit. Red in colour.

Closeburn: small grower, long flowering habit and recurring. Leaves small, dull, dark green, broadly ovate with pointed tip.

Bracts large, ovate with pointed tip; bright rosy red with coppery-coloured buds on opening.

Cinderella: double red (see 'Klong Fire' for complete description). Has variegated leaves.

Coconut Ice: syn. Margarita. Variegated- leafed variety which occurred as a bud-sport from 'Limberlost Beauty'. Bracts 'double', white with pink tips, and with cream and green foliage are particularly attractive. Medium size grower. Thorns medium and slightly curved. Leaves typically rounded as in the *buttiana* group.

Crystal Purple: typical of the *spectabilis* varieties; ovate furry leaves, vigorous growth. Bracts ovate and an iridescent, light purple. Seasonal flowering habit.

Cypheri: an old variety, rampant in growth; shining, dark green, pointed leaves. Bracts large, deep purple; flower is conspicuous and yellowish in colour. Thorns large and curved.

Daphne Mason: bud-sport of 'Killie Campbell' with the same very large bract and pendulous growth. Bracts lighter in colour, being coppery fading to pink. Very long flowering in a series of flushes; moderately vigorous. Thorns large and straight. Leaves long, oval, tapering to a long point at apex, and a long, slender petiole.

Daphne McCulloch: leaves dark green and glossy, margins reflexed; medium in growth habit and tends to grow out rather than up. Bracts round, large, somewhat 'blistered' looking and are a pure pink. Seasonal flowering. Thorns short and stout; ideal for ground cover and baskets.

David Lemmer: syn. Hensbergii. A vigorous open grower but bushes nicely with pruning. Leaves dark green, rounded, large and dull. Thorns not very prominent, being short and slender. Bracts broadly elliptic, large and bright red. Seasonal flowering habit.

Donyo: vigorous grower with large, light green leaves with wavy margins. Thorns long and straight. Bracts large and transparent, orange/pink and cover the plant all over in recurring flushes of flower. Sports occasional branches of light coppery red, which is the colour of its parent plant.

Double Yellow: syn. Aussie Gold, Carson's Gold. A yellow bud-sport from 'Klong Fire' commonly known as 'Carson's Gold'. Same in habit and appearance as other 'doubles'; bracts of clear bright yellow that fade to beige colour.

Easter Parade: medium-growing *glabra* cultivar with pointed pink bracts, very floriferous and has several long flushes of flower. Thorns fine and curved; leaves ovate to a pointed apex, light green and smooth.

Elizabeth: medium-growing variety with dark green, ovate leaves pointed at apex; new growth bronze. Bracts brilliant magenta-red, moderately large; young bracts coppery on opening. Thorns moderate and straight. Flower conspicuous, cream in colour. Long flowering periods several times a year.

Elizabeth Angus: vigorous growing; bright purple, large bracts; leaves dark green, glossy and tapering. Young stems puberulent; thorns stout, long recurved. Long flowering sessions several times a year. Flower yellowish, large and conspicuous.

Excelsior: *spectabilis*, vigorous, dense and bushy. Bract medium in size, clear light red. Leaves broadly ovate, furry to touch. New growth coppery. Thorns large, stout and recurved. Seasonal flowering.

Flame: loose upright but bushes well with periodic pruning. Leaves broadly ovate, dull, dark green; new growth distinctively red in colour. Bracts ovate with acute apex, medium size and good clear red. Flower is cream changing to orange as it ages. Thorns medium and straight.

Formosa: A typical *glabra* variety; dark green, pointed leaves, ovate with sharply pointed apex. Bracts small and pointed; light purple, finally turning to brown, and tend to stick on the plant. Flower conspicuous, tube very inflated and ridged. Very distinctive.

Freckleface: syn. Jamaican Orange. Bud-sport from 'Mrs McClean', has splashes of gold freckles in the centre of each leaf. Bracts typical *buttiana*, bright orange deepening to magenta overtones with age. Thorns medium straight. Flowers several times a year.

Gillian Greensmith: similar to Isobel but colour not as bright.

Gladys Hepburn: clear, pink, rounded bracts, vigorous grower, semi- deciduous in spring when it flowers.

Gloucester Royal: big-growing variety, *spectabilis* parentage obvious; large, dull, dark green leaves with pointed apex. Bracts large and the colour of a good claret. Seasonal flowering habit of long duration. Thorns large and strong and curved. New growth purplish red. Flower conspicuous and large.

Golden Summers: bud-sport from 'Penelope', less vigorous in habit. Leaves very golden in appearance, and with very large bunches of white bracts is a striking plant. Thorns medium and slightly curved.

Grimleyi: *spectabilis*; vigorous in habit. Leaves furry, broadly ovate with long, pointed tips. Bracts medium, pointed and hang in large pendulous bunches. Has a 'shaggy' appearance. Bract is orangey-red colour; seasonal in flowering habit. Thorns medium both in length and thickness.

Gwyneth Portland: one of the small shrubby types. Leaves ovate, glossy and have short petioles. Bracts medium, broadly ovate, bright yellow in colour; several long flushes of flowering. Thorns small and very few. New growth coppery.

Harlequin: syn. Thimma, Vicky. Bud-sport from 'Mary Palmer'. Leaves large as in parent plant and have a large splash of gold in the centre. Bracts as in 'Mary Palmer', as are all other characteristics. Tends to produce many green branches.

Harrissi: syn. Glabra Variegata. A variegated bud-sport from *B. sanderiana*. Less vigorous than parent and has light purple bracts. Tolerates more shade than other cultivars.

Hawaiian Gold: syn. Golden Glow, Millarii, Golden Queen. Typical *buttiana.* Leaves rounded and large; thorns medium and straight. Bracts broadly ovate, bright gold in colour fading finally to a pinkish gold. Vigorous and erect in habit. Flowering for several long periods in a year.

Hawaiian Orange: syn. Mrs McClean. Leaves broadly ovate, dark green, glabrous, erect and vigorous in habit. Thorns medium, stout and straight. Bracts medium, thin-textured, burnt orange in colour, finally fiery coppery red.

Hawaiian Scarlet: large seasonal, flowering red. Bracts large, rounded and brilliant red. Has long seasonal flowering on bare wood; very striking cultivar. Thorns long and strong; leaves rounded and dark green.

Isobel: syn. Isobel Greensmith. Loose, open and moderate in growth, finally becoming denser. Bracts fiery red; flowers in long periods several times a year. Bracts are ovate with very distinctive pointed appearance. Flowers open cream and become bright orange; thorns fine, long and curved. This variety tends to be rather spindly when very young. Leaves very dark green with pointed apex.

James Walker: brilliant red to magenta, vigorous

grower, bracts very large. Recurring flowering habit.

Jane Snook: syn. Dunbar, Durban, President. Leaves long and light green, with long petioles, compact and dense in growth habit; tends to be pendulous but does have some vigorous canes. Bracts in heavy bunches, large, pink and ruffled on the margins. Veining prominently green. Flower large and greenish cream. Flowering habit several long periods a year; thorns medium and fine.

Jayalaxshmi: syn. Kiri. Dense and bushy; leaves large, ovate, glossy, dull, dark green, rather thin textured, tapering to pointed apex; new growth very coppery. Thorns medium to long, slender and straight. Bracts almost round, thin textured; young bracts shading from reddish pink at base to red-purple to all-over reddish purple at maturity. Flowers conspicuous, cream. Pendulous heavy flowering in dry season. May defoliate when dried out. Thorns long and straight. Heavy seasonal flowering period.

Jennifer Fernie: syn. Beryl Lemmer, Mudanna. Medium grower, similar to Alba but bracts are broader and leaves narrower; lovely pure white.

John Lattin: erect leggy grower; leaves long, ovate medium green, glossy and pointed at tips. Bracts typical *glabra* shape but tapering to a long point at apex, palest lavender in colour, has an iridescent look. Flowers moderate in size, greenish cream. Thorns long and curved. Responds well to pruning and can be kept compact. Flowers several times a year for long periods.

Karega Bronze: syn. Margery Lloyd. Dull, dark green foliage, drooping in habit, but with strong canes. Leaves broadly ovate and slightly furry, sometimes an extra apex on leaves. Thorns medium to straight. Bracts large and thick, broadly ovate, pointed at apex, moderately large, opening copper through fiery red and finally magenta. Several long flowering periods a year.

Kayata: syn. Minyata, Shirley. Small-growing variety; in perpetual flower. Bracts medium to small, rich rosy red, twisted in appearance, typical *glabra* shape. Flowers conspicuous and white. Leaves medium to dark green, ovate, thick and shining. Thorns small and curved.

Kent's Seedling: large-growing variety, with long pointed leaves, somewhat furry in texture, medium to light green. Thorns stout, long, recurved. Bracts large, quilted, pointed and light purple.

	Long flushes of flowering several times a year.
Killie Campbell:	syn. Green light, Rose Amber. Big-growing pendulous variety; young plants lax. Thorns long and straight. Leaves dark green, long, ovate, margins wavy, tapering to long pointed apex. Petiole long. Bracts large, thin textured, ruffled in appearance with seductive colour changes from copper through red to magenta. Covers itself all over with masses of colour in recurring flushes. Flower large and conspicuous and does not open until late in bract development.
Klong Fire:	syn. Mahara Double Red, Carmencita, Manila Magic Red, Princess Mahara, Gladalan Red. One of the many names for the double red, one of the most popular and desirable of the bougainvillea cultivars. Large heads of 'double' bracts in recurring flushes. Can be kept small but is not a 'dwarf'. Typical *buttiana* in habit. Large, rounded, dark green leaves; stout medium thorns.
Lady Hudson:	representative cultivar of *B. peruviana*, long canes often bare of leaves especially when young; thorns fine and straight, bracts small, ruffled, pale pink.
Lady Mary Baring:	syn. Hawaiian Yellow. Bright yellow

bud-sport from 'Golden Glow'. Typical *buttiana*; erect growth, medium stout thorns, large, rounded, dark green leaves. Several flushes of colour a year.

Laidlaw: variety of *spectabilis* that is particularly seductive in colour of its very large bracts; the colour of the red blush on a peach. Seasonal flowering for a very long period. Large, ovate, furry leaves; large, curved thorns, and vigorous in growth habit.

Lateritia: syn. Dar-es-Salaam. An old cultivar of *spectabilis;* is the parent of many named and unnamed cultivars of Bougainvillea *spectabilis*. Typical *spectabilis;* not as vigorous as some. Bracts medium in size and brick-red in colour. Leaves medium size, furry to touch. Thorns medium and curved.

Lavender Queen: syn. Lavender Girl, Lavender Lady. Vigorous cultivar with glossy, light-green leaves; several flowering periods a year. Bracts large and light mauve; sometimes extra bracts in the group. Flowers creamy white, large and conspicuous. Thorns large, thin and curved.

Lesley's Selection: reported as bud-sport of 'Magnifica'. Flowers large, thin-textured, magenta-purple; big and conspicuous. Leaves long, ovate and glossy dark green.

Thorns long, strong and recurved. Very strong grower.

Limberlost Beauty: syn. Bridal Bouquet, Mahara Off White, Eastern Beauty, Eastern White, Tahitian Pink. Australian name for the 'Mahara Off-White', it has many synonyms. Typical *buttiana*; not as vigorous as other cultivars of the species. Bracts 'double' white with the tips of each small bract magenta. Thorns medium, leaves medium green, rounded.

Little Caroline: small-growing cultivar with brilliant fiery orange-red bracts that are pointed and twisted. Leaves small, dark green, pointed. Thorns long, thin and recurved.

Louis Wathen: syn. Orange King. One of the very early bud-sports from original 'Mrs Butt' or 'Scarlet Queen'. Bracts are rounded, orange in colour fading to bright fiery rose pink. Leaves are rounded, dark green and large. Thorns medium, stout and straight. Cultivar is readily distinguished by the incomplete flowers. Tends to be shy flowering for no apparent reason, probably in response to unfavourable conditions.

Magnifica: syn. Magnifica Traillii. The common purple with dark green glossy leaves. Vigorous growing to a dense bush.

Bracts thin-textured, ovate, brilliant glowing magenta. Flowers prominent, creamy white. Long flowering in the summer. Local name for it in Ecuador and Colombia is 'flor de verano' — summer flower. Thorns large, strong and recurved.

Mauve King: *glabra* variety with large, long, light green leaves; vigorous in habit. Thorns many, long and curved. Bracts thin textured, bright mauve, broadly ovate, tips reflexed. Flowers conspicuous, cream. Tends to grow very quickly and become unruly.

Meriol Fitzpatrick: syn. Dream. Similar to 'John Lattin' but bushier in habit. Leaves dark green, shining, elliptic. Thorns medium recurved. Bracts thin, broadly ovate, tapering to point; palest shimmering lavender with margins ruffled. Flower cream.

Mistress Columbine: variegated bud-sport from 'Mrs Butt'. Leaves gold-green with central green patch. Vigorous and has typical red bracts as 'Mrs Butt'. Thorns medium.

Mrs Butt: syn. Crimson Lake. Natural hybrid between *B. peruviana* and *B. glabra,* first discovered in 1910. Habit loose and upright, eventually becoming a very big shrub. Bracts medium in size and a good red in colour. Flower prominent and white with tinge of red. Thorns medium, stout and straight. Leaves large, rounded and dark, dull green.

Mrs Eva: compact-growing cultivar; prolifically flowering with bright mauve bracts several times a year. Leaves dark green, tapering to a pointed apex; thorns short, recurved.

Mrs E.W. Bick: typical *spectabilis*; vigorous, bushy with many long canes. Leaves dark green, furry to touch, tapering at each end. Thorns medium and recurved. Bracts ovate with acute apex, quilted in appearance and bright red. Flower prominent, cream.

Mrs H.C. Buck: syn. Mahatma Gandhi, Pacific Beauty. Hybrid seedling between *Bougainvillea glabra* and *B. peruviana*. Large growing; dense, bushy and with long strong canes. Thorns large, strong and straight. Leaves large, broadly ovate, medium to dark green, glabrous. Young shoots coppery. Bracts large, ovate, margins slightly wavy; deep rich magenta pink in colour. Flower large, pale cream and conspicuous; flowers in recurring flushes.

Mrs McClean: syn. Hawaiian Orange, Orange Glory. Bud-sport from 'Mrs Butt'; bright orange colour. Distinguished from 'Louis Wathen' by the complete flower tubes. Typical *buttiana* with large, rounded, dark green leaves. Erect habit of growth. Straight medium thorns. Flowers are cream, not conspicuous.

Mrs O. Perry: typical *spectabilis* but rather slow growing. Furry, ovate leaves, mid-green. Bracts ovate, orange, fading to magenta-pink as they age. Thorns small and slightly recurved. Flowers cream, conspicuous. Early seasonal flowering for long period.

Nina Mitton: bushy, dense habit; moderate in growth. Leaves thick, shining and mid-green, ovate with short petiole. Thorns short, thick recurved. Bracts small, almost round with sharply pointed apex; soft rose pink not changing with age. Flowers conspicuous, cream colour. Seasonal flowering habit, covering itself all over.

Orange Picot: syn. Hawaiian Sunset. Variegated form, slow growing, tends to be spreading in habit. Leaves small, deformed margins, streaked with cream. Bracts medium rounded, opening orange changing to rosy pink and finally pale pink; has multicoloured appearance. Thorns few, fine, straight. Flowers not conspicuous, opening late in bract development. Delicate; defoliates in cold weather, recovers, but the variegation is unstable. Very beautiful small-growing cultivar.

Pagoda Pink: syn. Los Banos Beauty, Double Phlox Pink, Miss Phillippine, Philippine Parade, Pink Champagne, Pink Delight, Tahitian Maid. 'Double' pink, typical *buttiana,* medium growing habit. Large bunches of bracts in recurring flushes. Leaves rounded and mid- to dark green; thorns medium and straight. No flowers because of 'doubling'.

Partha: syn. African Star, Indian Flame, Lemmer's Special. Tends to be sprawling in habit; ideal for banks and ground cover for large areas. Bracts thick, long, pointed, and slightly twisted; flame colour, opening coppery orange, through red to magenta. Leaves ovate, tapered at both ends, light to medium green and slightly rough to touch. Thorns medium, straight and strong. Flowers prominent, large and creamy white. Recurring flushes of flower; always some colour.

Penelope: syn. Shubra, Mary Palmer's Enchantment. Bud-sport from 'Mary Palmer'; large, vigorous-growing hybrid, dense and cascading. Leaves large, light to medium green and shining with wavy margins. Thorns large, strong, slightly curved. Bracts large, ovate, white with ruffled margins; faint flush of pink when growth slowed or shaded. Always flowering.

Phoenix: variegated-leafed version of 'Mrs Butt'; moderately vigorous in habit. Leaves very bright and variable, with gold, cream and green leaves; these are lovely with rich red of the bracts. Typical of *buttiana*, has rounded, large leaves, medium thorns and rich red bracts.

Picta Aurea: syn. Tropicus Splendour. Variable bud-sport from 'Speciosa Variegata'. Leaves splashed with gold and green; young shoots have purplish colour; thorns medium, strong and slightly curved. Puberulent leaves, canes as in all *spectabilis* cultivars. Bracts bright rich purple, large, ovate with prominent white flower. Seasonal, flowering for long period.

Pink Gem: typical *spectabilis*; vigorous, with long strong canes. Leaves large, ovate, tapering to pointed apex, furry to touch. Thorns many, short, slightly curved. Bracts large, ovate, quilted and bright rosy pink in colour. Flowers large, prominent and creamy white. Seasonal flowering habit, for very long period.

Poultoni: Compact, small to moderate growth, bushy. Leaves broadly ovate, pointed apex. Canes short. New growth reddish. Thorns few, small, slightly curved. Bracts moderately large, ovate with acute apex; open coppery red then to magenta-red, finally with bluish look. Flower conspicuous, cream.

Poulton's Special: syn. Clifton Carnival, Starfire, William Poulton. Moderate grower, sturdy and compact in habit. Leaves broadly ovate, margins wavy, thick, dark green and glossy. New growth reddish and slightly puberulent. Bracts large, broadly ovate, twisted and ruffled; rich rosy magenta. Flowers large, cream, distinctly ruffled.

Pride of Singapore: Seedling from 'Penang'; typical *glabra*, responds well to pruning. Leaves dark green, shining, ovate with definite pointed tip, edges slightly wavy, some brownish hairs on underside. Some leaves have extra lobe. Bracts small, bright purple, ovate, pointed tip, margins slightly wavy. Flowers prominent, cream and reflexed.

Purple Robe: large, strong, vigorous climber, dense and bushy; canes puberulent. Leaves dark green, glossy, ovate, pointed at tip; puberulent underneath. Bracts large, ovate with pointed apex; puckered. Brilliant rich purple, sometimes extra bracts and flowers give a 'tasselled' look. Flowers conspicuous, large, creamy white. Thorns large, strong and curved.

Raspberry Ice: syn. Tropic Rainbow. Variegated foliage, with cream margins, dark greyish-green centre to leaf. Leaves medium to small, ovate, tapered to pointed apex; margins wavy. Frequently sports shoots with no green in leaves. New shoots reddish. Bracts medium, ovate and bright red. Thorns short, thin and straight. Compact bushy grower; slow to grow but once established can grow very big.

Rosa Catalina: typical *spectabilis*; dense, bushy and vigorous. Leaves ovate, furry, tapering to a pointed tip; dark green. Thorns stout, medium length, slightly curved. Bracts medium, ovate with pointed apex; uniformly bright rosy pink. Flowers prominent, cream. Seasonal flowering habit.

Rosenka: bud-sport of 'Poultoni'; small growing and compact. Leaves small to medium, somewhat leathery, broadly ovate with pointed apex; light to mid-green. Thorns small and few. Bracts medium, broadly ovate, acute apex, margins slightly wavy; thin textured, changing from dusky orange on opening to dusky rose-pink at maturity. Flowers conspicuous and cream. Recurrent flowering habit.

Rubra Variegata: syn. Dauphine. Compact, rounded; typical *spectabilis*, somewhat furry to touch. Leaves large, ovate tapering to pointed tip. New growth reddish marbled with green, pink and cream. Variegation becomes less distinctive as leaves age. Bracts large, rosy red, ovate. Flowers conspicuous, cream. Flowering seasonal; begins early in season and continues to late.

Sanderiana: loose, upright with small dark green leaves, becoming dense. Thorns many, long, recurved. Bracts ovate, uniformly deep purple, pointed tips, veins green. Flowers conspicuous, creamy white.

Scarlet Glory: moderate grower with distinctly reddish new growth. Leaves dark green, broadly ovate, tapering at both ends; petiole short. Bracts small to medium ovate, light rosy red. Flowers small, conspicuous. Recurring, profuse flowering habit.

Scarlet O'Hara: syn. San Diego Red, Hawaiian Scarlet. Loose, upright, vigorous with strong canes. New growth dark wine red in colour. Leaves very large, rounded, dark green, thick textured and new growth slightly puberulent. Bracts nearly round; young bracts slightly orange shaded dark red, very large. Flowers conspicuous, cream and large. Thorns many, medium recurved. Seasonal flowering habit, often on bare stems in spring.

Scarlet Pimpernel: variegated-leafed version of 'Scarlet

O'Hara'; foliage very bright with streaks and patches of cream, light green and dark green; new growth reddish. Bracts large, bright red as in parent; growth moderately vigorous.

Scarlet Queen Variegata: syn. Rao. Beautiful creamy-white foliage, with patch of green in centre of leaf; very stable. Leaves small, rounded, pointed at apex, less vigorous than parent 'Mrs Butt'. Bracts red, with incomplete flowers as in 'Louis Wathen'. Grows quite well in bright shade, requires sun to flower well. Thorns slender, medium.

Show Lady: sparse, erect, scandent *glabra* cultivar; vigorous once established. Leaves light green, broadly elliptic, widest in the middle; petioles long. Bracts hang in drooping panicles; palest lavender-pink; broadly elliptic with acute apex. Flowers moderately large, cream. Thorns long and slender.

Singapore Pink: rounded, shrubby, glabra cultivar with long elliptic light green leaves tapering to pointed tip. Bracts large, lavender-pink, elliptic and reflexed. Flowers prominent, cream. Thorns short, not prominent. Has tendency to defoliate in cold weather.

Singapore White: syn. Clifton Moonlight. White-bracted form of Singapore Pink, bracts tend to stay on when faded.

Smartipants: Medium to tall, upright plant with small leathery leaves, internodes very short and leaves look crowded. Thorns short, stubby and blunt, bigger on strong canes. Bracts small and closely packed; magenta-red in colour. Flowers prominent, white and small. Not attractive unless kept regularly pruned to encourage multiple new growth.

Silver Magenta: small, dark green, glossy leaves, broadly elliptic, shining and tapering to pointed apex. Bracts small, light purple, elliptic, tapering to long pointed apex. Thorns small, curved, fine. Flowers prominent, creamy white. Dense bushy habit, strong grower.

Snow Cap: syn. Mary Palmer. Bi-coloured bud-sport from 'Mrs H.C. Buck'. Large, medium-dark smooth green leaves, broadly ovate tapering to point at apex. Bracts large, ovate and variously coloured deep pink to white; some are parti-coloured. A truly spectacular sight in flower. Recurring flushes of heavy flowering. Thorns large, strong, recurved.

Speciosa: typical *spectabilis*; vigorous, dense and rounded. Leaves dull, dark green, ovate, tapering to a short pointed apex. Slightly furry to touch. Thorns medium, stout and curved. Bracts large, rich deep purple, margins slightly wavy. Flower very prominent, cream. Seasonal flowering.

Speciosa Variegata: variegated bud-sport from 'Speciosa'. Leaves variable, usually creamy margin, irregularly shaped, with large patch of greyish green in centre, otherwise the same as Speciosa.

Spectabilis: the name which describes variable plants within the species. Typical leaf shape with varying degrees of hairiness. Dense seasonal flowering habit in the dry season.

Splendens: rampant variety of *spectabilis,* with very hairy leaves, canes and thorns. Leaves large, broadly elliptic to ovate, dark green, hairy, tapering to pointed apex. Bracts very large, ovate with rounded apex, light purple. Thorns long, strong and recurved. Flower conspicuous and bright creamy yellow. Seasonal flowering habit.

Srinivasia: vigorous, cascading, dense. Leaves very large, mid to dark green, smooth, ovate, tapering sharply to a pointed apex. New growth bronze. Thorns large, stout and slightly recurved. Bracts very large, ovate, with acute apex, margins wavy; brilliant rose pink to red. Flowers conspicuous, cream. Recurring flowering habit.

Tango: syn. Miss Manila, Manila Hybrid. Vigorous, cascading, dense. Leaves medium to large in size, somewhat ovate, light to medium green; new growth coppery. Thorns medium to strong, straight. Bracts large, whorled, rounded at apex, slightly ruffled, veining prominent. Young bracts orange opening to clear orange and fading to light pink, giving a multicoloured look. Recurring flowering habit. Flowers large and prominent; cream.

Temple Fire: dwarf, shrubby variety, growing to about a metre tall and wide. Leaves small, broadly ovate, shortly pointed at apex; margins slightly wavy. Bracts broadly ovate, pointed apex, uniformly reddish purple in colour. Buds slightly more coppery. Thorns small, short, slender.

Temple Fire variegated: same as above, less vigorous, has variegated foliage.

Texas Dawn: syn. Purple King, Robyn's Glory. Bud-sport from 'Mrs Butt'; same rounded leaves and loose, open habit. Thorns many, long, stout, slightly recurved. Bracts rounded, light purple-pink, uniform in colour; no change.

Texas Dawn variegated: bud-sport from 'Texas Dawn'; less vigorous than parent. Attractive marbling and streaking of cream and grey-green in leaves.

Thai Gold: syn. Roseville's Delight, Mahara Orange, Golden Glory, Golden Doubloon, Tahitian Gold. As with other 'doubles' there are many names used in marketing. Habit loose, upright, open. Responds well to clipping. Leaves dark green, ovate, rounded, coming to sharp point at apex. Bracts small in clusters of 20–40 to a cyme; burnt orange in colour fading to carmine pink. Flowers nil due to 'doubling'. Bracts tend to brown and stay on bush.

Thai Gold variegated: same as above; leaves streaked and marbled with light green and cream.

Thomasi: syn. Rosea. Dense, vigorous, typical *spectabilis*. Leaves ovate, large, medium to dark green, hairy. Thorns large, strong and curved. Bracts very large, carmine pink, broadly ovate with acute apex; veining prominent. Flowers large and conspicuous, cream.

Tomato Red: *spectabilis* seedling; habit dense, vigorous, pubescent. Seasonal flowering. Leaves ovate, velvety to touch, apex acute; young growth coppery. Bracts medium size, broadly elliptic, light brick red, fading lighter. Flower conspicuous, cream.

Treasure: stiff, upright, bushy-leaved, medium in growth habit. Leaves waxy, thick, shining, ovate with acute apex; margins slightly wavy. Thorns short, thick, blunt; larger on strong canes. Bracts densely crowded, small, pointed, changing from a copper-peach colour through magenta to purple-magenta. Flowers not conspicuous, white.

Turley's Special: typical *spectabilis* cultivar; dense, vigorous. Leaves medium size, ovate, tapering to pointed apex, velvety to touch. Bracts medium, broadly elliptic with acute apex; cherry red. Flowers conspicuous, cream. Thorns medium to large, curved.

Vera Blakeman: erect and shrubby, with stiff growth; medium grower. Leaves medium thick, waxy in appearance, mid-green, ovate, tapering to pointed apex. Bracts densely crowded, small, pointed, uniformly magenta-red. Flowers conspicuous, white.

Wallflower: typical *spectabilis*; densely shrubby, vigorous. Leaves dark, dull green, ovate, velvety to touch. Thorns medium, curved. Bracts oval, apex rounded; rich bronze-red colour. Flowers conspicuous, cream.

William Poulton: syn. Poulton's Special, Starfire, Clifton Carnival.

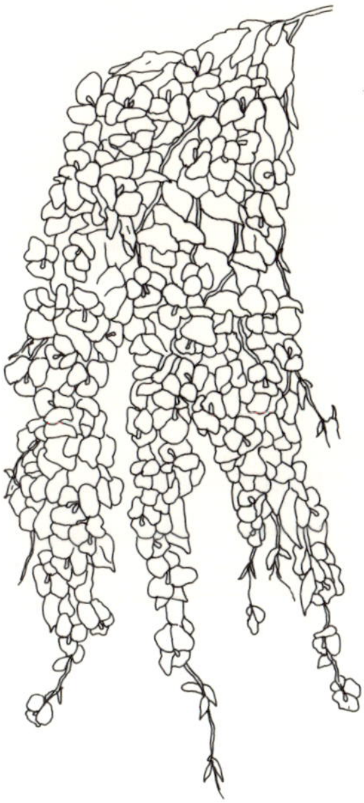

Chapter Four

GROWING AND USING BOUGAINVILLEAS

Whether you wish to grow your bougainvillea in a pot or basket, up a tree or over a wall; as a shrub or a tree, there will be a bougainvillea cultivar which will suit your requirements perfectly.

Bougainvilleas are very plastic and adaptable plants, and can be trained to grow as you wish. However, many of the modern cultivars have different growth habits and size. This means less effort in attaining and maintaining the effect you want if you choose your cultivars carefully. In the following pages you will find detailed information on how to raise and train your bougainvilleas.

Selection of the individual plant is important — small plants are generally more fragile than bigger ones. The plant should be sturdy and have thick, white roots which should emerge from the drainage holes — or at least be visible. If the plant you are buying is straight from glasshouse conditions, it is advisable to provide some shelter until it is hardened off.

CULTIVATION

It is good practice to follow the adage 'water, mulch and fertilise'. Water well. By this I mean that you should soak the ground thoroughly and then soak it again when the surface of the soil has dried out. Water more frequently, when the weather is hot, dry and windy — sometimes twice daily if you have your plants in pots. In cold weather water less frequently, because bougainvilleas do not like to have cold wet leaves. Water your plants in the morning during winter. If the leaves of bougainvilleas are wet on a cold night they can drop off.

Mulch your plants well with rotted animal manures, spent mushroom compost, compost, old straw, old seaweed from which all salt has been thoroughly hosed, bagasse, leaf mould, pine bark or wood chips.

Soil

Soil science is a complex and specialised subject, but you need to know something about it because the well-being of your plants depends on the quality of the soil they grow in.

Soils are classified as varieties of clays, loams and sands. Loam is the best to grow plants in because it combines clay, silt and sand together with humus to make a friable (crumbly-textured) soil. The most important factor in creating soil which will crumble is the presence of humus, which is produced from organic matter by micro-organisms living in the soil. Soil organisms are vital to help form soil; algae, bacteria, fungi, insects and worms all work to build and improve your soil. Humus in soil is more advantageous to plants than its small proportionate amount would indicate. A sound rule of thumb in gardening is to be generous with organic manures and careful with inorganic fertilisers.

Plants grow best in crumbly soils like loam because nutrients and oxygen are freely available to their roots. The greater the depth of soil, the deeper the roots will be able to penetrate and the greater the amount of nutrients and moisture available. The result is a vigorous plant which can withstand periods of drought.

Water

Water is essential to plant growth, most of it being absorbed through the root hairs, although a little is absorbed through the leaves. The importance of water may be appreciated when it is realised that 70-90 per cent of the plant's weight is water.

Water is not only used in the manufacture of plant foods, it is also used in transpiration, and when transpiration exceeds water absorption, wilting results. Excessive dryness causes root death, which retards plant growth.

Bougainvilleas are broad-leaved plants and being vigorous growers need plentiful water when making new growth. For a good display of flowers it is essential that the plant makes continual new growth. No new growth — no flower.

Should you let your bougainvilleas dry out completely the small roots will dry up and die, but only water your plants when the surface soil is dry. There is no hard and fast rule about when to water, such as every second day or once a week. The amount of water needed depends on soil type, climatic conditions, size of plant, whether it is in a pot and the amount of humus and other moisture-retaining matter surrounding the plant. *Look at your plant* — it will tell you if it is distressed and needs a drink. Water deeply, drenching the root area. Small amounts of water will restrict growth of the root system and will cause failure to thrive. Light watering makes the plant grow surface roots, whereas deep watering helps the roots to penetrate the soil deeply.

Light

Bougainvilleas love the sun. They are best as outdoor plants, but they can be grown and will flower successfully in glasshouses; glasshouses mimic the tropical climate. Either very bright sunrooms or window alcoves with the sun on them most of the day are suitable. The bracts will be a lighter colour than those grown in full sunshine, but still beautiful and attractive.

Position

The position and preparation of the site selected for planting are most important to get the best results from your bougainvillea. Choose an open sunny position preferably sheltered from cold winds; bougainvilleas which grow in full sun are healthy and flower prolifically. They will survive in shade but only flower sparsely if at all, and grow spindly and leggy in habit.

You should think about how your young plant will look when it is mature and needs more space. Bougainvilleas are long-lived plants and some varieties can grow to prodigious size given optimum conditions.

Regular pruning controls the size and shape. The majority of active growth occurs from the middle to the end of summer, when many strong watershoots are produced; this is the time to work on your bushes to bring them back to shape.

Selection of varieties

Cultivars have different growth habits and can produce a variety of effects. Select small cultivars for smaller areas such as 'Temple Fire' which grows slowly to about one metre and is shrubby in habit and long flowering. 'Little Caroline' is small but more scandent, and less compact than 'Temple Fire'. 'Kayata' blooms perpetually and is a compact small-growing plant. Other compact cultivars include 'Gwyneth Portland', 'Rosenka', 'William Poulton', 'Dorothy McCulloch', 'Closeburn'. (See Ch. 3 for descriptions.) Most bougainvilleas are big growers and that is why special mention is made here of small-growing cultivars.

Site preparation and planting

Bougainvilleas tolerate most soils but must be planted out carefully. Good preparation gives them a good start in life, which helps them towards strong and healthy growth. The hole should be at least half as deep again and twice as wide as the container that the plant is in. Fill the hole with water to assess drainage and if it acts like a reservoir, break away the sides to promote drainage. Bougainvilleas hate to have wet feet and their roots die if they are left to sit in a water hole. Fill around the plant with a mixture of good sandy loam, animal manure, compost and slow-release fertilisers, either in pellets or granules.

When you are planting out either far from hoses and taps or where your plants will get infrequent watering, you can use moisture-retaining agents which are available from most nurseries. Mix reagent to a gel and place in the bottom of the hole, just under the root ball of the plant. These agents, such as Agrisoke, Polysoak and others can hold up to 4000 times their volume of water; this can be a saviour in times of drought. Moisture retainers will last through the growing season and at least until the plant has established strong roots. This does not mean, however, that you never have to water the plant — it means that the plant is likely to survive less frequent watering in the early stages after it is planted out.

If you keep your plants in pots for several weeks before you plant them out, remember that they have been well nurtured in the nursery before you bought them so be sure and check them daily. Place them in a sunny position and make sure they are watered thoroughly each day. When you plant them out ensure that the root ball is moist. Allow all potted plants to drain thoroughly after they are watered and before you begin to plant them out or pot them, otherwise the weight of the water in the soil could cause it to collapse when the plant is transferred, and damage the roots.

Do not plant too deeply; the plant should be at about the same level in the ground as it was in the container. The soil around the newly-planted bougainvillea may be firmed by gentle pressure with the feet but do not stamp on it with hobnail boots; tread gently and softly. Apply a suitable mulch to the whole area around the new plant and water thoroughly, preferably with a sprinkler.

Spacing

Give your plants enough room to grow to maturity without being crowded. Most varieties are comfortable 3 metres apart; less space is necessary for medium growers and less again for the small plants.

Staking

Bougainvilleas tend to develop bulky crowns, so it is advisable to tie them to a solid hardwood stake. Use short stakes when you want cascading growth, as in window boxes and down banks. The heads of bougainvilleas can become quite large and such bushes can snap off at ground level in strong winds.

Transplanting and aftercare

Select and prepare the new site carefully in advance; do not transplant bougainvilleas in either autumn or winter. Spring is the perfect time. Remember not to skimp on site preparation otherwise you may forever be trying to put it right. Plants frequently fail after they are transplanted, either because their roots have been damaged or the gardener failed to provide adequate care to help the plant to become re-established. Prune the top of mature plants back about ⅓ to ½, and cut in a circle around the tree with a sharp spade at about the circumference of the new drip-line, or about 30cm (12") for each 2.5cm (1") of trunk thickness. Keep the spade and the cut vertical, not at an angle. This cut should be made several weeks before the plant is moved and the plant should have been fed with an agent such as *Formula 20* to stimulate feeder root growth.

Take great care when the final movement of the plant is done.

Stay wires will help to hold big transplants in place; they should not wobble while they are establishing a new system of roots. Water thoroughly every other day for about 5-6 weeks and spray the foliage frequently to further reduce water loss.

Mulch

Mulch helps to retain moisture in the soil. Spread it 10-15cm (4–6") deep around the plant but keep it at least 10cm (4") away from the trunk or stem to prevent damage by fungus and decay.

Sprinkle some nitrogenous fertiliser (urea, nitram, sulphate of ammonia) over the mulch if it contains decomposing vegetable matter. This prevents leaching of nitrogen from the soil. Do not use lawn clippings as a mulch because they form a mat and stop water penetrating to the soil. Decomposed composted lawn clippings make excellent mulch.

Foliar fertiliser

Foliar fertilisers are either sprayed or poured over the plant in solution so that the nutrients can be absorbed through the leaves. A small amount (e.g. 1 teaspoon to 10 litres or 2.25 gallons) of household detergent or white oil helps to stick the fertiliser on the leaves and promotes absorption. Foliar fertilisers can be used together with other fertilisers and can be applied every 2 to 4 weeks in the growing season. Many commercial liquid fertilisers are available — fish emulsion, liquid seaweed, Thrive or Zest will suit very well.

Iron chelates, potassium nitrate, magnesium sulphate (1 teaspoon to 4 litres or 1 gallon water) could be included in alternate feedings.

Pruning

Bougainvilleas should be lightly pruned after the end of the flowering period. Unwanted watershoots should be removed after the rainy season, otherwise further flowering could be inhibited. Very hard pruning is generally not recommended although some varieties tolerate it well. Bougainvillea *spectabilis* cultivars do not appear to mind heavy prunings, but it is far better to keep your bougainvilleas in shape by regular light pruning.

Bougainvilleas are good climbers, and use the thorns in the axils of the leaves to get a grip. Each branch usually terminates in an inflorescence where the flowering shoots develop in place of the thorns. When flowering is complete normal vegetative climbing growth proceeds.

Holiday care

All gardeners face the common problem of how to care for their plants when they go away on holiday. Perhaps a friend or neighbour may be kind enough to offer to do the watering. If not, check your local paper for enterprising people who do this for a fee which is usually quite reasonable.

Alternatively, you could use 'tree bags'; these are large plastic bags which hold about 10 litres (2.25 gallons) of water and have an adjustable wick outlet to control the volume released. The bag is placed at the base of the plant and the water will trickle out for up to 3 weeks. The bags need to be well covered with mulch or the water released will be hot and can damage or kill the roots. Do not use these bags as permanent fixtures because they can waterlog the ground or cause the roots to be directed only to the small area where the soil is moist. The old adage of flooding regularly and allowing to dry — but not completely — is still the best to keep your plants healthy; this keeps the roots expanding outwards and deeper, seeking water and nutrients.

An automatic watering system is a good investment and is the way to ensure proper plant maintenance. They also save a lot of time, and the advent of small computerised home watering units is wonderful! They can be programmed to deliver the exact amount of water required for your particular garden. Timer taps are less expensive but quite useful as they will automatically turn off after the preselected time has elapsed.

Cultivation in cool climates

The secret of successful gardening is to grow plants in as close to their natural habitat as possible. Bougainvilleas are hot climate plants and suffer in the cold, but they can be successfully grown.

Do not plant them out into the ground when the soil temperature is too low. Good plants can be grown in 20cm (8") and 30cm (12") pots. Plastic absorbs the heat better than concrete or clay and is much lighter, which is an attribute when the plants have to be moved around.

The potting medium should be open, free draining and rich in humus. Do not let the pots stand in saucers full of water in the winter months and, as the weather shows signs of becoming cold, move the plants to a protected area which is favoured by plenty of winter sunshine.

Do not place your plant beneath a tree for protection from frost, because the shady conditions will be equally harmful. Bougainvilleas are best wintered in a glasshouse or, alternatively, in a sunny, glassed porch or a sunny room. Keep them there until warm weather begins.

Glasshouses can be freestanding or attached to a house. They can be made of plastic, fibreglass or glass. The glasshouse must receive the maximum amount of sunshine and it should be positioned accordingly. When moving plants from a glasshouse to outside sunshine, it is necessary to 'harden off' the plant, otherwise the leaves and flowers could be scorched. The reason for this is that the cell walls in the leaves are thinner in plants kept in glasshouses so that they can absorb the maximum sunlight for photosynthesis.

Plants grown in glasshouses are often called 'soft', compared with 'hard' plants in the open. Keep glasshouse plants for several weeks in a 'halfway house' before you move them outside; this will give the cell walls time to thicken and strengthen. The light-dappled shade of a tree sheltered from strong winds is excellent.

1

2

3

4

5

B. spectabilis cultivars:

1. 'Mrs E. W. Bick'
2. 'Turley's Special'
3. 'Pride of Zimbabwe'
4. 'Laidlaw'
5. 'Thomasi'

6

7

B. glabra cultivars:

6. 'Alba'
7. 'Formosa'
8. 'John Lattin'
9. 'Singapore Pink'
10. 'Magnifica'

8

9

10

11

12

B. buttiana cultivars:

11. 'Mrs McClean'
12. 'Doubles'
13. 'Mrs Butt'
14. 'Apple Blossom'
15. 'Hawaiian Gold'

13

14

15

16

Variegated cultivars:

16. 'Raspberry Ice'
17. 'Harlequin'
18. 'Freckleface'
19. 'Cinderella'
20. 'Golden Summers'

17

18

19

20

21

22

24

Dwarf cultivars:

21. 'Poultoni'
22. 'Temple Fire'
23. 'Rosenka'
24. 'Gwyneth Portland'
25. 'Kayata'

23

25

26

27

Hybrid cultivars:

26. 'Killie Campbell'
27. 'Isobel'
28. 'Daphne Mason'

28

29

30

31

Hybrid cultivars:

29, 30. 'Donyo'
31. 'Penelope'
32. 'Snowcap'

32

33

34

Hybrid cultivars:

33. 'Tango'
34. 'Lavender Girl'
35. 'Scarlet O'Hara'
36. 'Poulton's Special'

35

36

Frost protection

Bougainvilleas need to be protected from the frost when they are young, although they are generally fairly frost resistant. The best protection is to cover them up at night to trap daytime warmth and ground heat. Bubble plastic sheeting makes the best blanket as it lets more light in, but an ordinary plastic sheet will do. Make the plastic shelter large enough so that the leaves do not touch the plastic itself and risk of sunburn is reduced.

USING BOUGAINVILLEAS

Potted plants

Many hybrid bougainvilleas make excellent pot plants, having inherited many desirable attributes of their parent species including moderate growth rates, large showy bracts and multiple divided flowering cymes. These features along with recurrent heavy flowering make the hybrids wonderful plants to grow in pots. Larger cultivars can also be grown in pots provided they are controlled by pruning.

Bougainvilleas are gross feeders and need a rich compost which includes some peat moss, composted animal manures and slow-release fertiliser either in the form of granules or pellets. Top up the pots with compost and fertiliser every 3 months.

A routine of pruning, feeding and watering followed by 6 weeks in flower can result in 4 main flushes of flower each year. If several plants are treated in this fashion but at different times, then you can always have a bougainvillea in full flower. Frequent watering simulates natural, heavy rain and when followed by a dry period induces flowering.

Prune and shape your plants after they flower, keep them

to about a metre high, and remove all the twiggy growth. Feed each pot with a balanced fertiliser that is high in potash and contains trace elements, at the rate of one tablespoon to a 30cm (3 gallon) pot, and soak well with water to ensure maximum uptake of nutrients. In very hot weather when new growth is rapid plants may need to be watered twice each day. Watering should be gradually reduced but sufficient to prevent wilting. Foliar fertilisers can be applied at this time at about 7–10 day intervals.

The vigorous growth of new shoots during the rainy season can be a problem because it can induce nutrient deficiency and leaves will turn yellow (this is chlorosis). This can be resolved by several applications of sequestered iron and magnesium sulphate (Epsom Salts).

Your plants should be in full flower about 7 weeks after pruning and will continue to flower for about 6 weeks. Once flowering starts apply a high potash fertiliser and resume heavy watering. Prune your plants again once flowering is finished, and repeat the cycle of feeding and watering. Remove any roots which appear in the drainage holes of potted plants. Remember that bougainvilleas are gross feeders, and potted specimens need topping up with rich compost every few months. With care bougainvilleas will grow and flower successfully in pots for over 10 years.

Repotting

Potted bougainvilleas will need repotting every 3 or 4 years, even though they can be maintained for longer periods in pots. The procedure is to prune the top back by about ½ to ⅓, turn the pot on its side and ease the root ball out. A strong jet from the hose will help. Prune the root ball back by about ⅓ and repot into rich compost. Again, this should be done in spring rather than later autumn or winter.

There are many commercial potting mixes available in

supermarkets and garden centres. For bougainvilleas choose a loose friable mix, to which you will need to add some peat moss and fertiliser. Water-retaining elements are available and are an excellent additive. Slow-release fertiliser is ideal for potted plants. The same principles apply to whatever size pot you happen to be using.

John Innes Compost is very suitable for growing bougainvilleas, using No.l for baby plants with new young roots to Nos.2&3 for older plants.

This compost originated from the John Innes Horticultural Institute in England after many years of research into plant requirements. One of the essential components is John Innes Base Fertiliser, which consists of:

2 parts hoof and horn
2 parts superphosphate
1 part sulphate of potash

John Innes Compost No.l is made from:

7 parts sterilised and sieved loam
3 parts peat moss
2 parts soars sand,
measured by volume

To each bushel (20 litres) of No.1 Compost add 22g (0.8 oz) garden lime and 120g (4.25 oz) John Innes Base Fertiliser.

To use John Innes Compost No.2 double the quantity of John Innes Base Fertiliser for each bushel (20 litres) of Compost No.l.

With John Innes Compost No.3 you treble the amount of John Innes Base Fertiliser added to each bushel of Compost No.l.

John Innes Compost No.l is a standard mixture for potted plants and Nos.2&3 provide for progressively richer composts.

Fertilisers for potted plants

Fertilise potted plants regularly and top them up with mulch. Spray the leaves with appropriate fertilisers to keep your potted plant well fed. Remember potted plants have limited soil and much nutrient is leached away when you water them.

Balanced fertiliser mix:

2 teaspoons sulphate of ammonia
3 teaspoons superphosphate
1 teaspoon potassium sulphate or potassium nitrate
½ teaspoon sulphate of iron
¼ teaspoon magnesium sulphate (Epsom salts)

This covers an area about 60cm (2 feet) in diameter and gives a good boost to plant growth. Apply this fertiliser about every 3 to 4 weeks if you intend to use it regularly.

Standards

Bougainvilleas grown as 'standards' are a truly magnificent sight and are well worth the time and effort needed to achieve the result. They can be grown in the ground or in large pots.

Standards should have a single stem, but sometimes several main stems which have been kept clean of shoots will help to form a more substantial umbrella of foliage. The plant should look formal and when fully in flower, it will show as a superb ball of colour. A substantial stake is needed until the trunk is thick enough to support the crown; this could take some years.

You can sometimes buy standard bougainvilleas in nurseries. They are usually 3 to 4 years old and have a smallish crown, but if they are either potted up or transplanted into the ground they should grow quickly into good-sized specimens.

If you wish to train your own standard from scratch select a plant of good size — specimens in 200mm (8") or larger pots with one or more strong watershoots. Proceed as follows:

1 Plant into either a larger container or the ground and make sure that you attend carefully to all the procedures in the section on planting out. (See p.59)

2 Set either a stout stake or pipe into the ground or the pot, and plant the bougainvillea beside it. A circular, triangular or square frame at the top of the stake makes an excellent support for the top growth but is not essential.

3 Select one long shoot and run it up to the height you require (about 2 metres or 6 feet is a good height) and top it. Tie the shoot to the stake at several places; make it tight enough to support the plant but not so tight that the plant will be strangled. Clip off the thorns, leaves and any lateral shoots.

Now that the stem is free of thorns it will be easier to rub off any shoots which grow later.

The intention is to promote the growth of strong lateral branches which radiate out from the top of the watershoot. Keep heading back these chosen branches as they grow (nip out the tips when the shoots are 7-10cm or 3–4 inches long) and remove spindly shoots until a solid crown of branches is achieved. Now shoots can be allowed to grow and then they can be wrapped around and tied back into the framework of the crown. Once the desired shape and size is achieved, the crown should be regularly pruned and spindly growth cleared out after the flowering season. Bougainvilleas are long-lived plants — up to 100 years. So it is well worth the effort and time you put into making your bougainvillea into a standard plant.

When repotting standards, the same principles apply as those used to repot any other bougainvilleas. Some people have been known to turn out the plant, beat and shake out all the soil, cut all roots back to 'stumps' and repot successfully. As a general rule this treatment is not recommended — you can easily kill your precious plant!

Plants can be grown successfully in large plastic pots and are much easier to handle when repotting. Large clay pots are aesthetically more pleasing and also help to insulate the rootball from heat. Plastic pots absorb a lot of heat when exposed to the sun.

Standards should be grown in either heavy concrete or clay pots to help prevent them blowing over in strong winds.

All bougainvillea cultivars make suitable standard specimens because of their pendulous habit of growth.

The cultivars 'Treasure', 'Sanderiana' and 'Vera Blakeman' look very good as formal standards.

Shrub or bush

Keep the plant cut low so that the trunk will become thick and strong to support the grown shrub. Prune back long branches to maintain shape and remove watershoots which emerge from the crown. Once you have achieved the desired height and spread, prune side branches selectively to maintain size. Trim the 'underskirts' and remove the lowest canes to avoid a 'hard-pruned' look, but do not worry if you are forced to prune your plant hard, because new growth will compensate for the loss very quickly.

Hedges

Bougainvilleas makes secure formal or informal hedges. Plants should be spaced about 1 to 1½ metres (3–5 feet) apart depending on the variety; smaller cultivars can be planted closer together.

To get best results adhere to the same general rules recommended previously when planting out. Good soil rich in humus, which has been mixed with a generous amount of complete fertiliser in both the slow release and quick action forms, helps the hedge to grow.

B. glabra cultivars with compact habits of growth, small leaves and a long flowering period, and which respond well to clipping, make excellent formal hedges.

Great visual impact is achieved by planting the hedge with one variety together like *B. glabra* 'Sanderiana' for a purple hedge, *B. glabra* 'Alba' for a white hedge and *B. glabra* 'Easter Parade' for a lavender-pink hedge.

The more upright cultivars, the *buttiana* group, either in one or in mixed colours, make lovely informal hedges. In these, when the canes come out in summer, they flower at the ends and then progressively all along the cane, which is a wonderful sight.

Take care to use one variety in the hedge to preserve uniformity of effect. The buttiana group come in a range of colours, from the original red, through orange, yellow, pink and white tinged with pink; and forms such as the doubles in red, orange, yellow, pink and white with a tinge of pink.

B. spectabilis grows into larger shrubs and has seasonal flowering habits. It makes solid blocks of colour when in full bloom. It grows into dense formal hedges which respond well to clipping.

To establish a hedge, cut away the top growth to control the height and encourage lateral spread of the plant. Each year allow a little more top growth until you have achieved the desired height.

Tie the strong shoots along the length of the hedge and let their new shoots rise to fill the hedge and make a strong framework.

Once the hedge is established it is important to remove all strong new canes at their source or they will spoil the shape. Light pruning after flowering is finished will keep the hedge in shape. Thereafter remove irregular canes and branches, dress annually with a slow-release fertiliser and a good thick layer, 15cm (6") of aged chicken litter, stable manure or composts. A further light dressing of a fertiliser which is high in potash in late summer helps to improve flowering.

Pergola

Plant a robust specimen of bougainvillea next to your pergola, tie a strong shoot to the end upright and remove all other shoots. This main shoot will grow rapidly and extend above the pergola roof. When the shoot is about a metre above the pergola, bend and tie it to the top centre framework. The lateral shoots which then grow should be directed to form a network of branches which cover the top of the pergola. Trim the shoots from time to time to keep the pergola neat and tidy, and prune after flowering; make sure that only one shoot is retained to the branches on the pergola roof.

Some branches will need to be removed occasionally to reduce the density of growth on top of the pergola. The colour of the light shining through the bracts is superb, so it is advisable to keep leafy growth to a minimum.

Espalier

Plants which are grown flat, either on a wall, fence or framework, are called espaliers. Bougainvilleas are beautiful when grown in this manner, particularly against a sunny wall.

Prepare the site to be planted in the usual way and position your plant as close to the wall as possible. Attach a suitable vertical branch to the wall and let it grow as high as required. Lateral branches should be allowed to develop at appropriate spaces so that the wall may be seen, as this is part of the whole effect. Remove all unwanted shoots and all forward growth, and fix the chosen lateral branches into position while they are still flexible. You can achieve any shape you desire but the overall effect should be controlled and formal.

Clothing a steep bank

Bougainvilleas make good cover on banks. A fine display will be assured if the following rules are observed:

1 The bank must be in full sunshine.

2 Plant at the base of the bank — again heeding all the requirements recommended in the section on planting out (see p.59).

3 Train one or two stems up to the top of the bank and then take them horizontally in either direction. Rub off the shoots, leaves and thorns from the stems. Now the horizontal branches should put out pendulous laterals which will drape down the face of the bank to wonderful effect.

Through a tree

The bigger, rampant bougainvillea varieties like 'John Lattin', 'Meriol Fitzpatrick', 'Scarlet O'Hara' and 'Thomasii' make spectacular cascades when grown up to the top of trees.

Select and plant a specimen with a strong stem, close to a tree. Stop it from branching until it grows at least half way up the tree. The shoots should now grow rapidly up through the canopy, seeking light, and once on top it will put out lateral shoots which will fan out and flower in the sun. The plant must be fertilised and watered regularly because the tree will demand much of the available food and water.

Indoors

Bougainvilleas can be grown indoors provided they are given enough light; there should be enough for the plant to cast a shadow. They can be successfully grown in greenhouses and in very bright sunrooms in temperate climates. Indeed, once the bracts are formed, they are tolerant of moderate light changes and changing temperatures, and will continue to give a good display even if you move them around.

Bonsai

Bonsai is a Japanese word which means 'planted in a tray'.

Bougainvilleas are excellent subjects for the Bonsai enthusiast. To grow Bonsai plants is a fascinating art in itself and there are many good and inexpensive books on the subject, and often classes as well, if you wish to attempt it.

Bonsai are generally classified according to size, attitude, number of trunks growing from a single root, the number of trees in a group planting and the kind of base on the plant.

Sizes are:	miniature	—	under 15cm (6")
	small	—	15–30cm (6–12")
	medium	—	30–60cm (1–2 ft)
	large	—	over 60cm (2 ft)

The same rules apply to bougainvilleas as to any other species being made into a Bonsai. You will be absolutely delighted when your miniature bougainvillea bursts into brilliant colour. The more pendulous varieties which tend to drape naturally lend themselves to cascade styles of Bonsai.

PESTS AND DISEASES

Bougainvilleas are favoured, both ecologically and economically, because they are relatively free of pests and diseases. You do not need to spray for insects and diseases to grow beautiful flowering plants. This is desirable considering the huge amounts of chemicals generally used for insect controls which are toxic and pollute the environment.

Bougainvilleas grown in full sun, which is their normal habitat, have thick cell walls. This protects them from attack by disease-causing organisms. Plants grown in the shade have thinner cell walls and are therefore more vulnerable to attack.

Leaf spot

In prolonged wet conditions in the tropics, leaf spot can be a problem, even for bougainvilleas, and when the conditions are very severe, leaf spot can account for 80 per cent of leaf fall in young plants.

The major cause of leaf spot worldwide is the bacteria *Pseudomonas stizilobii*, which is often accompanied by a fungal leaf spot which likes the same conditions.

Spray at the first signs of disease. It is essential to follow the instructions on the packet exactly and at the recommended strengths.

The fungi which cause disease are: *Cercosporidium bougainvillae; Colletotrichum dematum bougainvillae; Gladosporum arthrinoides*.

The appearance of small reddish rounded spots on the leaves is a characteristic early sign of infection by *Pseudomonas stizilobii*; the spot is usually surrounded by a 'halo' of pale green which merges into normal leaf colour. Spots rapidly expand to become irregular dark patches which are bounded by small veins and when the attack is severe, the patches become almost black and distort the young leaves, which leads to severe defoliation. As the dry season approaches, the new growth can still become infected but usually less severely so. Leaves which remain on the plant until the following year provide the source of infection the next time conditions are right. The disease is transmitted in water and can be prevented by removal of all the dead leaves and by reducing crowding between plants. Plants grown in greenhouses watered by overlapping sprinklers are particularly susceptible to spread of the disease.

Cool, showery nights and late afternoon watering often result in leaves which remain wet overnight and can also increase the susceptibility of your plants to the disease. Spray with fungicides to control the problem. These are effective for long periods and will control a wide range of diseases, in addition to fungi. They are sold under various trade names but the active ingredients are listed below:

benomyl
captan
maneb
mancozeb
zineb

Mites

Marginal leaf curl, where the leaves cup and distort, is caused by mites. The condition is not usually severe and by the time the distortion is apparent the mites have been and gone. It is thought the mites secrete a hormone in their saliva which they inject into the leaves to interfere with their growth. Mite infestations usually occur during warm humid weather and new growth which appears at other times will be normal.

Spray severe cases regularly at intervals of 10-14 days with a systemic acaricide (e.g. maldison) and thereafter at the onset of warm weather. This will stop further infestation. If the disease is not severe, either ignore it or cut away the offending branches.

Aphids

Aphids often infest new growth and flowering shoots, which they can distort and sometimes kill. Infestation can become particularly severe in humid glasshouse conditions.

Spray with maldison, which also controls mites, scale and grasshoppers. Maldison has a short residual action but it is not very toxic to animals and humans. Again adhere to all the instructions on the label.

Other insects

There are some insects which can be a nuisance in the USA. These are controlled by insecticides. One of these is the soft scale *Coccus hesperidium*, which attacks plants grown in both greenhouse and open garden. In Florida, the caterpillar *Ascioides gordinalus* and the beetle *Amphericus cornatus* Pallas can also be problems. The beetle is commonly known as the bougainvillea beetle.

In the past, ants were controlled by toxic chemicals with long residual action. These have now been removed from the market. Check with your local nursery about current methods to control ants. Dust insecticides are useful when repotting ant-ridden specimens; dust the new soil, the old root ball and the top of the pot.

Earthworms in pots

Earthworms are a nuisance rather than a pest because they

convert potting mix into a heavy sludge; rotenone (Derris dust) at the rate of 28g (1 oz) of 1 per cent dust to 1 square metre or square yard of soil will evict them.

PROPAGATION

It is most rewarding to propagate your own plants. Most bougainvilleas 'strike' quite easily and those varieties which are more difficult to grow can either be air-layered (marcottage) or layered. Bougainvilleas can also be grafted and budded.

Cuttings

Hardwood — 150–200mm (6–8") long and 10–15mm (⅖–⅗") in diameter taken in late winter are cut on an angle just beneath the node at the basal end of the cutting, and just above the node at the top end. The cutting is either dipped or dusted with root promoting hormones and planted to about ⅔ of its length into a 50/50 mixture of sand and peat moss in a pit in the open. Take many more cuttings than you need because only about one in three will grow into a good plant. It can take up to 3 months before you get really good root and leaf growth, but you will then have a strong and sturdy plant.

Semi-ripe cuttings — taken from the previous season's growth in spring when the new bud shoots are showing signs of growth. The cuttings should be 150–200mm (6–8") long, as thick as a pencil, and treated like the hardwood cuttings.

Eight to ten cuttings are placed in a 120mm (6") pot filled with 50/50 coarse sand and peat moss and kept either in a greenhouse or a warm bush-house. The cuttings are ready to pot on when strong aerial growth and thick white roots show through the drainage holes. Upend and remove the plant from the pot carefully. Gently break open the soil mass, taking care not to damage the roots. Small bougainvillea plants have very delicate and brittle roots, which need careful handling. Separate the cuttings and plant them into 120mm (6") pots. Place in a warm sheltered position until the baby plant is recovered and growing well. When the plant has become well developed, pot up into a larger container. At the beginning of winter it is safer to leave this further repotting until the spring; in any case do not overpot small plants.

Layering

Many clones which do not root easily from cuttings can be successfully layered and propagated. Layering is a simple method for propagation of small numbers of plants, which does not need either special skills or equipment. Layering allows the propagation of larger plants in a shorter time than growth from cuttings.

Root formation during layering is stimulated when the flow of nutrients and auxins from the shoot tips to the roots is interrupted; the natural stem flow of auxins is from apex to base. Auxins and nutrients build up where the stem is cut and cause roots to form there. Root formation is facilitated by darkness, so the point of layering should be either buried or mounded with soil.

Soil which retains moisture and is full of humus helps roots to grow, particularly when the cut stem has also been treated with root-promoting hormones.

The stem has to be wounded because the injury causes the hormones to accumulate, which encourages roots to form. Make a slit about 35mm (1 ½") long through the centre of the stem just below a node or leaf junction and insert a small foreign body to keep the cut edges apart. Cover the layer with plastic weighed down with stones to stop soil from blowing and washing away.

Once the layered stem starts to grow, cut it free from the parent plant and pot it up carefully, taking care not to damage roots.

Marcottage or air-layering

Marcottage or air-layering is a good method to propagate plants; pencil-thick stems give the best results. Select a branch and cut it on an angle just below a node, ¾ through its thickness. Dust the cut with hormone rooting powder and keep the edges open with a piece of gravel, coarse sand or other suitable material about 2mm (1⁄12") diameter. Wrap a generous amount of thoroughly moistened sphagnum or peat-moss around the cut, cover with plastic film, tie the centre and each end to keep the moss in firm contact with the cut surface. The layer is successful when roots show in the plastic cocoon and new growth starts to appear at the top; this usually takes about a month. If the moss appears to be drying out, untie the top and pour in a little water. Support the layered branch because the strength of the cut stem is much weakened. Pot up the new plant in the usual fashion.

Grafting

Grafting is the art of joining areas (the cambium layer) of a cutting to an understock to grow as one plant. The cambium layer is the tissue which lies between the bark and the central wood of a plant.

Grafting plants can be traced back to ancient times. Mixtures of wet clay and dung were used in those times to cover the graft unions.

A successful graft aims to fit two pieces of living plant tissue together so that they will unite and grow as one plant. The short piece of stem material which is to form the leafy canopy of the plant is called the scion. It should be of the desired cultivar and free of disease. The stock or rootstock is the lower part of the graft and could be a seedling or a rooted cutting of an existing established plant. Usually a desirable cultivar which is difficult to propagate because it produces a poor root system of its own is grafted onto a stock which grows a vigorous root system. To graft successfully, the scion and rootstock must be compatible; the cambiums of stock and scion must be in close contact with each other, and the cut surfaces held together tightly by wrapping. The wound needs to heal rapidly if the scion is to be supplied with nutrients and water by the rootstock.

All cut surfaces should be covered with grafting wax once the join is made, to prevent moisture loss. Care of grafted plants must be maintained carefully after grafting i.e., support the scion, remove shoots from the rootstock and put the graft in a humid environment so that the scion does not dry out.

Some bougainvillea cultivars which have either little or no chlorophyll in their leaves are almost impossible to grow from cuttings and therefore need to be grafted onto a vigorous rootstock to be propagated.

Budding

Another aspect of growing bougainvilleas as a hobby is the growth of several varieties on a single plant to make exciting and colorful displays.

The technique is called budding, which involves the insertion of a bud (the scion) under the edges of a T-shaped cut in the bark of the plant (the rootstock) to which you wish to add the new variety. A clean sharp knife should be used and it is a good idea to have a few practise runs.

Make a 20mm (¾") T-shaped cut in the bark of the recipient plant and insert the donor bud under the flaps, tie with either raffia or grafting tape so that there is no movement. Seal the area with grafting wax or other similar compound to exclude air. If the bud is still green and healthy looking after 3 weeks it will probably be a successful union.

The bud should be selected from the current year's wood, and it is important the piece chosen does not dry out. Should you take a large cutting with a number of eyes in it, cover it with a wet cloth while you make the incision in the rootstock. Leave about a centimetre above and below the eye when you cut it from the stem, and remove thorns and pithy pieces of wood from behind the eye by gently squeezing the bud piece. Slip the bud, right way up, in behind the flaps in the T-cut and bind securely to prevent movement. Seal with grafting wax. If your first efforts are not successful, keep trying until you have mastered the technique.

Nutrition

Plants, like all living things, need food to survive. Bougainvillea, although a hardy plant, is no exception. Plants construct much of their food by way of photosynthesis from relatively simple materials like water and carbon dioxide which they combine, in the presence of sunlight, to make sugars. Sugars, salts (minerals in solution) and various compounds absorbed from the soil provide the requirements to build plant structures. Fertilisers contain many of these essential nutrients in organic and mineral form.

Plants absorb the substances they need in soluble form through their roots. Plants starve when there is a shortage of any one of their nutrients and individual deficiencies show up as different signs and symptoms.

Try to learn the subtleties of these signals from your plants before jumping to conclusions. Also, remember that the elements missing in the plant may not necessarily be lacking in the soil; it may be that they are just not in a form which is available to the plant.

The availability of nutrients is closely tied to soil pH. This is a measure of acidity on a scale ranging from 1 to 14 where 1 indicates extremely acid conditions, 7 is neutral and 14 is extremely alkaline. Soils range in pH from about 3 in peat-bogs to 10.5 in arid, alkaline soils. Most plants grow best at pH 6 to 7 and at these pH values all the minerals which are essential to plant growth are soluble and available.

Bougainvilleas tolerate a wider pH range than many plants, but they may show iron and magnesium deficiencies (chlorosis), especially in pots, just after flowering, at the end of winter and in the tropics after prolonged rain.

Plants must have water, otherwise no matter how much nutrient is available in the soil, the plant will wither and fail to thrive. It is far better to flood your pots and garden plants with water than to ration the amount of water given each or every other day; this restricts and stunts root growth and reduces plant vigor.

As a good guideline to how much water is needed, bear in mind that the amount of root area approximately equals the amount of aerial growth. Large plants in pots should be watered more frequently because their roots are restricted by the size of the pot.

Common inorganic deficiencies include:

Nitrogen (N)	older leaves turn a yellowish green with veins sometimes reddish. Severe deficiency shows as stunted young leaves and slender, hard young twigs
Phosphorus (P)	Veins and leaf stalks turn red to purple and the leaf blade becomes mottled yellow to blotchy brown
Potassium (K)	edges on older leaves become purplish, generally preceded by tip-burn; eventually the younger leaves are affected

Magnesium (Mg)	older leaf blades become either blotched yellow or tan with veins remaining green
Zinc (Zn)	can be similar to magnesium but leaves may be stunted, crinkled and their growth crooked
Sulphur (S)	younger leaves turn entirely yellow, with the veins a brighter colour than the leaf blade
Molybdenum (Mo)	mottling over whole leaf but little pigmentation; leaves cupped with distorted stems
Manganese (Mn)	all younger leaves remain green, blades turn yellow and later brown blotches appear over entire leaf
Calcium (Ca)	dead areas appear in young tender leaves at tips and margins. Terminal buds remain either smaller than usual or shrivel and die. Calcium becomes unavailable if the soil pH is greater than 7.8
Boron (B)	terminal buds appear similar to those suffering calcium deficiency; leaf stems brittle and leaf bases turn yellow
Iron (Fe) and **Aluminium** (Al)	often occur when soil is too alkaline; leaf blades either pale or yellow, larger veins remain green but smaller veins turn yellow; later edges of leaves turn brown.

When the major elements (N, P and K) are lacking, an application of a standard chemical fertiliser should overcome the problem. If minor elements are missing, specially mixed formulas of soluble trace elements may be used. Single-element additives, such as iron chelates, are also available.

Remember that too little is better than too much. Many healthy young plants have been over fertilised and killed. Natural products, such as liquid seaweed, fish emulsion, compost and animal manures, can supply all elements needed for plant growth. Either a soil test or leaf analysis can be done to establish the proper treatment needed.

Manures

Comparative Values of Animal and Poultry Manures

Source	**Nitrogen (percent)**	**Phosphoric Acid (percent)**	**Potash (percent)**
Cattle	0.20	0.17	0.10
Horse	0.44	0.17	0.35
Sheep	0.55	0.31	0.15
Pig	0.60	0.41	0.13
Poultry	1.10	0.85	0.56

Poultry manure is richest in elements but lacks bulk and humus. Manure makes a wonderful mulch which is full of essential nutrients; fresh manure is best but always keep it away from the base of plants. 'Weathered' manure has had much of the nutrient leached out of it.

Many affected plants do not grow well and have poorly developed roots; it is sometimes possible to save these plants by potting them back to a smaller pot. Often it is better to discard the affected specimen and start again.

When buying your plant check the drainage holes of potted plants to ensure that there are strong roots showing through.

Chlorosis

Chlorosis is the term used to describe the yellowing of leaves commonly caused by mineral deficiency; most commonly iron, magnesium and nitrogen.

Most bougainvilleas with chlorosis respond favourably to watering with iron chelates together with magnesium at the recommended rate at 10-14 day intervals until the leaves become green.

GENETICS AND BREEDING

It is usual to have a double set of chromosomes, all in pairs, which is referred to as the diploid state ($2\underline{n}$). Haploidy ($\underline{n}$), triploidy ($3\underline{n}$), tetraploidy ($4\underline{n}$) and various other forms of multiple sets of genes are also seen.

Fertility and interbreeding

Bougainvilleas have $\underline{n}=17$ chromosomes and the majority of cultivated varieties are diploid, ($2\underline{n}=34$). Some, however, are triploid ($3\underline{n}=51$) and there are natural as well as induced tetraploids, ($4\underline{n}=68$).

In self-pollination, pollen is transferred from the stamens of a flower to the stigma of the same flower. Cross-pollination means transfer of pollen from one plant to the flower of another. In general, pollination is successful only between plants of the same species, but hybrids can result when pollen successfully fertilises plants of allied species.

Self-pollination is prevented in many flowers by devices such as opening and discharge of pollen before the stigma of the same flower is receptive. These flowers are said to be 'self-sterile'. The value of self-sterility is to promote cross-pollination and therefore to increase variation within the species. Varied genetic content has survival value for plants in different and changing environments.

Inbreeding has resulted in a largely infertile range of *Bougainvillea* cultivars. Induced tetraploidy has restored fertility to some, but like the fertile diploid cultivars, they are self-sterile and can only reproduce with other fertile cultivars.

Flowers, which are specialised reproductive organs, are central to the survival and evolution of the higher plants. Flowering plants transfer genetic material between genetically similar individuals. Some specialisation occurs into male and female parts to different degrees, depending on the species.

Like most flowering plants, *Bougainvillea* has a brightly coloured part (the flowering bract or inflorescence is actually a set of specialised leaves rather than petals of a flower) to attract insects that serve to take pollen from the protruding anthers to the stigma on top of the ovary, as described below. This occurs within one bush and from plant to plant.

The genetic information that dictates the nature of the plant and its growth, development, reproduction and the business of survival from day to day is carried in the form of genes, which act as little 'messengers' grouped together in long strands called chromosomes. The form and number of each chromosome is identical in organisms with the same heredity, and within different cells of the same individual (with rare exceptions). Reproduction means copying the genetic material and packaging it for exchange with another organism that may have slightly different genes on otherwise identical (and therefore compatible) chromosomes.

Genetic manipulation is the subject of ongoing research, especially in India, and opens new possibilities such as smaller-growing varieties — perhaps even a thornless variety may be possible.

The issue of fertility is clouded by a lack of comprehensive knowledge, inconsistent nomenclature and reports on different cultivars and the occurrence of variations in response to climatic and environmental change.

For example, it has been reported in India that *B. buttiana* and all the bud-sports examined on this hybrid have sterile pollen and seed (Sharma & Battachaya (1960); Zadoo et al. (1974-82) — but seedlings from *B.* 'Mrs Butt' have been reported from Kenya.

It is well known that seed-set and fertility are largely influenced by climate (usually favouring warm dry conditions) and it is possible that a planned breeding programme may only achieve what has occurred naturally in the past.

Interspecies variation

It is generally held that bougainvilleas are self-sterile and that most modern varieties, certainly of those in widespread commercial horticulture, are completely sterile. The occurrence of new varieties from natural interbreeding is limited and they now come chiefly from bud-sports. Even a fertile specimen produces only a handful of seed from thousands of flowers. Seed is commercially available mostly imported from India, but it invariably includes only varieties of *Bougainvillea spectabilis*. Seedlings which I have grown from naturally-fertilised *B. spectabilis* cultivars have developed into plants with a wide variety of colours and bract sizes, and with differing degrees of furriness on the foliage. There will be much unknown variation among plants grown from seed taken from different places. It is noteworthy that seeds brought in to Australia and grown in several different locations have resulted in plants which show bracts with only subtle differences in colour, and with the habits and basic characteristics of existing varieties. Unfortunately, many of these seedlings are given new names and are claimed as unique varieties without adequate attention to the true distinguishing features of leaf, flower, thorn type, habit and bract colour.

It is equally regrettable that varieties which appear among groups of cuttings are renamed and sold as bud-sports when they clearly belong to an already-named variety.

Seedlings of *Bougainvillea glabra* show a very much wider range of differences in size and shape of leaf and bract than do *B. spectabilis*, but the colour range remains in the mauves to purples.

B. glabra and *B. spectabilis* are similar in essential form and structure; the major difference is that *B. spectabilis* is hairy. Both species show considerable variability. *B. peruviana* differs from *B. glabra* and *B. spectabilis* in leaf shape, division of cyme, shape of flower tube, and there is no variability within the species; indeed there is only one representative cultivar, called *B. peruviana* 'Lady Hudson' (syn. 'Princess Margaret Rose').

Bud-sports

A spontaneous and unpredictable genetic change in an organism gives rise to a mutation which is generally permanent and heritable.

In the plant world, changes in the basic genetic information (a true mutation) or changes (sometimes temporary) in the way that information is expressed may lead to differences in leaf and flower — these are called either 'sports' or 'bud-sports'.

Many of the cultivars known in the genus *Bougainvillea* come from 'sports', particularly from the more complex hybrids, usually those which include *B. peruviana* as one of the parent species. Well-known examples include *B.* X *buttiana* 'Mrs Butt' (*glabra* X *peruviana*) which sports two different colours (pink, orange, gold and white), and has developed leaf variegations, double-flower forms and varieties with incomplete flower parts.

'Mrs H.C. Buck' (*B.* X *specto peruviana*) has produced a

bi-coloured mutation and white and variegated leaf forms.

Numerous other sports are known, but some have uncertain parentage. It is interesting that apparent mutations vanish as mysteriously as they appear, and that colour changes are usually lighter (e.g. red to orange to gold, pink, and white) and may even by seen serially in successive sports. Occasionally, a sport back to original colour may be seen (e.g. 'Thai Gold' sports back to 'Klong Fire').

Manual pollination

Take a flower bud that is almost ready to open, cut the upper half of the tube and remove some of the anthers; remove the remaining anthers with forceps but leave the stigma attached. Cover the flower overnight, dust pollen from the desired parent onto the stigma and re-cover the flower to prevent casual pollination.

Pollinate selected flowers early in the morning when the weather is dry. Label the potential seed flower with information about the experiment.

Seeds become ripe in about 30 days and thereafter germinate quickly. The seed is viable for some time.

Flower structure

Bougainvillea flowers are always in groups of three and each one is subtended by a brightly-coloured bract.

Bracts have two functions: they attract pollinators; and they act as a wing for mature seed.

The structure of the flower is strange. It is a single tube with a slight constriction in the middle between a swollen base and a funnel-shaped upper part which opens into a five-rayed star. The flower tube is marked by five ridges along its length which support the points of the terminal star.

There is either a white or a cream wrinkled membrane which joins the five points of the star to form the conspicuous part of the flower. A few stamens may be seen from the top inside the flower tube.

INDEX OF CULTIVAR NAMES

Cinderella
Clifton Carnival — Poulton's Special, Starfire, William Poulton
Clifton Moonlight — Singapore White
Closeburn
Coconut Ice — Margarita
Crimson Jewel — Barbara Karst
Crimson Lake — Mrs Butt
Crystal Purple
Cypheri
Daphne Mason
Daphne McCulloch
Dar-es-Salaam — Lateritia
Dauphine — Rubra Variegata
David Lemmer — Hensbergii
Donyo
Double Yellow — Aussie Gold, Carson's Gold
Doubloon — Golden Doubloon, Mahara Orange, Thai Gold, Roseville's Delight, Golden Glory, Tahitian Gold
Dream — Meriol Fitzpatrick
Dunbar — Jane Snook, Durban, President
Durban — Jane Snook, Dunbar, President
Easter Parade
Eastern Beauty — Beauty, Bridal Bouquet, Cherry Blossom, Eastern White, Mahara Off White, Thai Queen, White Haze, Limberlost Beauty, Tahitian Pink
Eastern White — Beauty, Bridal Bouquet, Cherry Blossom, Eastern Beauty, Mahara Off White, Thai Queen, White Haze, Limberlost Beauty, Tahitian Pink
Ecuador Pink — Lady Hudson, B. peruviana
Elizabeth
Elizabeth Angus
Excelsior
Fair Lady — Blondie, Hugh Evans
Flame
Formosa

Freckleface — Jamaican Orange
Gillian Greensmith
Glabra Variegata — Harrissi
Gladalan Red — Carmencita, Klong Fire, Mahara Red, Manila Magic Red, Philippine Red, Princess Mahara
Gladys Hepburn
Gloucester Royal
Gold Queen — Hawaiian Gold, Golden Glow, Millarii
Golden Doubloon — Doubloon, Golden Glory, Tahitian Gold, Mahara Orange, Thai Gold, Roseville's Delight
Golden Glory — Doubloon, Golden Doubloon, Mahara Orange, Thai Gold, Roseville's Delight, Tahitian Gold
Golden Glow — Hawaiian Gold, Millarii, Gold Queen
Golden Summers
Greenlight Rose Amber — Killie Campbell
Grimleyi
Gwyneth Portland
Harlequin — Thimma, Vicky
Harrissi — Glabra Variegata
Hawaiian Gold — Golden Glow, Millarii, Gold Queen
Hawaiian Orange — Mrs McClean, Orange Glory
Hawaiian Scarlet — Scarlet O'Hara, San Diego Red
Hawaiian Yellow — Lady Mary Baring
Hawaiian Yellow (variegated)
Hensbergii — David Lemmer
Hugh Evans — Blondie, Fair Lady
Indian Flame — Partha, African Star, Lemmers Special
Isobel — Isobel Greensmith
Jamaica White — Apple Blossom, Audrey Grey
Jamaican Orange — Freckleface
James Walker
Jane Snook — Dunbar, Durban, President
Jayalaxshmi — Kiri
Jennifer Fernie — Beryl Lemmer
John Lattin
Karega Bronze — Margery Lloyd

Kayata — Minyata, Shirley
Kent's Seedling
Killie Campbell — Greenlight Rose Amber
Kiri — Jayalaxshmi
Klong Fire — Carmencita, Gladalan Red, Mahara Red, Manila Magic Red, Philippine Red, Princess Mahara
Lady Hudson — B. peruviana, Ecuador Pink
Lady Mary Baring — Hawaiian Yellow
Laidlaw
Lateritia — Dar-es-Salaam
Lavender Girl — Lavender Lady, Lavender Queen
Lavender Lady — Lavender Girl, Lavender Queen
Lavender Queen — Lavender Girl, Lavender Lady
Lemmers Special — Partha, African Star, Indian Flame
Lesley's Selection
Limberlost Beauty — Beauty, Bridal Bouquet, Cherry Blossom, Eastern Beauty, Eastern White, Mahara Off White, Thai Queen, Tahitian Pink, White Haze
Little Caroline
Los Banos Beauty — Mahara Pink, Pagoda Pink, Philippine Parade, Pink Delight, Pink Champagne, Tahitian Maid
Louis Wathen — Orange King
Lutea Variegata — Speciosa Variegata
Magnifica — Magnifica Traillii
Magnifica Trailii — Magnifica
Mahara Off White — Beauty, Bridal Bouquet, Cherry Blossom, Eastern Beauty, Eastern White, Limberlost Beauty, Thai Queen, Tahitian Pink, White Haze
Mahara Orange — Doubloon, Golden Doubloon, Thai Gold, Rosevilles Delight, Golden Glory, Tahitian Gold
Mahara Pink — Los Banos Beauty, Pagoda Pink, Philippine Parade, Pink Champagne, Pink Delight, Tahitian Maid
Mahara Red — Carmencita, Gladalan Red, Klong Fire, Manila Magic Red, Princess Mahara, Philippine Red
Mahatma Gandhi — Mrs H.C. Buck, Pacific Beauty
Manila Hybrid — Miss Manila, Tango

Manila Magic Red — Carmencita, Gladalan Red, Klong Fire, Mahara Red, Princess Mahara, Philippine Red
Margarita — Coconut Ice
Margery Lloyd — Karega Bronze
Mary Palmer — Snowcap, Surprise
Mary Palmer's Enchantment — Penelope, Shubra
Mauve King
Meriol Fitzpatrick — Dream
Millarii — Gold Queen, Hawaiian Gold, Golden Glow
Minyata — Kayata, Shirley
Miss Manila — Tango, Manila Hybrid
Mistress Columbine
Mrs Eva
Mrs E.W. Bick
Mrs H.C. Buck — Mahatma Gandhi, Pacific Beauty
Mrs Butt — Crimson Lake
Mrs McClean — Hawaiian Orange, Orange Glory
Mrs O. Perry
Mrs A.T. Stephenson — Silver Magenta
Nina Mitton
Orange Glory — Mrs McClean, Hawaiian Orange
Orange King — Louis Wathen
Orange Picot — Rosenka variegata
Pacific Beauty — Mrs H.C. Buck, Mahatma Gandhi
Pagoda Pink — Los Banos Beauty, Philippine Parade, Pink Champagne, Pink Delight, Mahara Pink, Tahitian Maid
Partha — Indian Flame, African Star, Lemmers Special
Penelope — Shubra, Mary Palmer's Enchantment
Philippine Parade — Los Banos Beauty, Pagoda Pink, Pink Champagne, Mahara Pink, Pink Delight, Tahitian Maid
Philippine Red — Carmencita, Gladalan Red, Klong Fire, Mahara Red, Princess Mahara, Manila Magic Red
Phoenix
Picta Aurea — Tropicus Splendour
Pink Champagne — Los Banos Beauty, Mahara Pink, Pagoda Pink, Philippine Parade, Pink Delight, Tahitian Maid

Pink Delight — Los Banos Beauty, Mahara Pink, Pagoda Pink, Philippine Parade, Pink Champagne, Tahitian Maid
Pink Gem — Cannellii
Poultoni
Poulton's Special — Clifton Carnival, Starfire, William Poulton
President — Jane Snook, Durban, Dunbar
Pride of Singapore
Princess Mahara — Carmencita, Gladalan Red, Klong Fire, Mahara Red, Manila Magic Red, Philippine Red
Purple King — Texas Dawn
Purple Robe
Rao — Scarlet Queen Variegata
Raspberry Ice — Tropic Rainbow, Strawberry Ice
Rosa Catalina
Rosea — Thomasi
Rosenka
Rosenka variegata — Orange Picot
Roseville's Delight — Golden Doubloon, Doubloon, Thai Gold, Mahara Orange, Golden Glory, Tahitian Gold
Rubra Variegata — Dauphine
Sanderiana
San Diego Red — Scarlet O'Hara, Hawaiian Scarlet
Scarlet Glory
Scarlet O'Hara — San Diego Red, Hawaiian Scarlet
Scarlet Pimpernel
Scarlet Queen Variegata — Rao
Show Lady
Shubra — Penelope, Mary Palmer's Enchantment
Silver Magenta — Mrs A.T. Stephenson
Singapore Beauty — Singapore Girl, Singapore Pink
Singapore Girl — Singapore Pink, Singapore Beauty
Singapore Pink — Singapore Beauty, Singapore Girl
Singapore White — Clifton Moonlight
Smartipants
Silver Magenta

Snowcap — Mary Palmer, Surprise
Snow White — Alba
Speciosa
Speciosa Variegata — Lutea Variegata
Spectabilis
Splendens
Srinivasia
Starfire — Poulton's Special, Clifton Carnival, William Poulton
Strawberry Ice — Raspberry Ice, Tropic Rainbow
Surprise — Mary Palmer, Snowcap
Tahitian Gold — Mahara Orange, Doubloon, Golden Doubloon, Roseville's Delight, Golden Glory, Thai Gold
Tahitian Maid — Pagoda Pink, Mahara Pink, Pink Delight, Pink Champagne, Phillipine Parade, Los Banos Beauty
Tahitian Pink — Bridal Bouquet, Cherry Blossom, Eastern Beauty, Limberlost Beauty, Eastern White, Thai Queen, White Haze, Beauty, Mahara Off White
Tango — Miss Manila, Manila Hybrid
Temple Fire
Temple Fire Variegata
Texas Dawn — Purple King
Texas Dawn Variegata
Thai Gold — Doubloon, Golden Doubloon, Golden Glory, Mahara Orange, Roseville's Delight, Tahitian Gold
Thai Gold Variegata
Thai Queen — Beauty, Bridal Bouquet, Cherry Blossom, Eastern Beauty, Eastern White, Mahara Off White, White Haze, Tahitian Pink, Limberlost Beauty
Thimma — Harlequin, Vicky
Thomasi — Rosea
Tomato Red
Treasure
Tropic Rainbow — Raspberry Ice, Strawberry Ice
Tropicus Splendour — Picta Aurea
Turley's Special

Vera Blakeman
Vicky — Harlequin, Thimma
Wallflower
White Haze — Beauty, Bridal Bouquet, Eastern Beauty, Eastern White, Mahara Off White, Thai Queen, Tahitian Pink, Limberlost Beauty, Cherry Blossom
William Poulton — Poulton's Special, Starfire, Clifton Carnival

GLOSSARY

Acuminate — tapering to a point
Acute — sharply pointed but not drawn out
Adnate — joined to
Adventitious — in other than the usual place
Air-layering — *See* Marcottage
Aneuploid — not having an exact multiple of the haploid set of chromosomes and therefore genetically unstable
Angiosperma — the group of plants which possess flowers
Anther — pollen-bearing top of stamen
Apex — tip of organ (e.g. 1eaf)
Apical — relating to the apex
Apiculate — with a short, stiff point
Arborescent — becoming tree-like, woody
Asexual — propagates without sex, so no new genetic material is introduced
Attenuate — becoming narrow, tapered
Aurea — golden
Auxin — plant hormone which regulates growth. Used for stimulating formation of adventitious roots
Axil — the point just above the leaf where it rises from the stem

Bagasse — residue after extracting juice from sugar cane or beet
Basal — at base of organ
Beta-cyanins — red-purple pigment found in plants
Beta-xanthins — yellow-orange pigments found in plants
Blade — the expanded, flattened part of a leaf
Bract — modified leaves intermediate between flower and normal leaves, often coloured

Calyx — outer circle or cup of floral parts (usually green)
Cambium — cylindrical layer of actively dividing cells which give rise to secondary (woody) tissues, causing increase in

periclinal

girth of stem
Centrosperma — central seed
Chimera — organism with two or more genetically distinct tissues
Chlorosis — yellowing of leaf
Chlorophyll — complex green pigment found in green plants, active in the process of photosynthesis
Chromosomes — microscopic rod-like bodies in the plant cell, made up of genes and bearing the 'blueprint' for reproduction
Ciliate — fringed with eyelash-like hairs
Clasping — with the leaf or bract surrounding the stem
Compound — similar parts aggregated into a common whole
Concave — curved inwards; hollowed out
Connate — united in one body
Convex — curved outwards
Cordate — heart-shaped
Coriaceous — leathery
Corolla — complete circle of petals
Crenate — with teeth rounded, scalloped
Cultivar — special genetic form originating in cultivation
Cuneate — wedge-shaped, triangular
Cuspidate — tipped with a short, stiff point
Cyme — type of inflorescence in which the flower stem elongates from a series of lateral branches

Defoliate — lose leaves/foliage
Dehisce — to spontaneously separate leaves, branches, flowers
Decurrent — leaf blade extends down petiole
Deltoid — triangular
Diploid — having two sets of chromosomes
Dissected — several or more times cleft into small segments
Distal — at the far end
Divided — separated at base

Doubling — increased number of petals or bracts, beyond the norm

Elliptical — oblong with widest point at centre
Elongate — drawn out in length
Emasculate — remove masculine flower parts
Endemic — not found outside a restricted area or country
Entire — margin without toothing or division

F1 hybrid — first-generation hybrid obtained by artificial cross-pollination between two genetically dissimilar parents.
F2 generation — second generation of a given cross. Usually obtained through self-pollination of the F1 hybrids so that there is genetic variation among individual plants
Floriferous — bearing flowers
Formosa — finely handsome
Friable — crumbly texture
Fusiform — spindle-shaped, rounded and tapering from the middle towards each end

Glabrous — smooth, not hairy or rough

Haploid — having one set of chromosomes
Hirsute — hairy, with long rather stiff hairs
Hybrid — plants resulting from a cross between parents that are genetically different

Inflorescence — the flowering part of a plant
Internode — space between two nodes
Involucre — bracts surrounding flowers on their supports

Laciniate — slashed into narrow, irregularly-pointed lobes
Lanceolate — lance-shaped, tapering towards tip
Lenticel — raised, corky projections on young bark giving vent to breathing pores

Limb — the border or expanded part of the corolla above the throat
Linear — narrow and flat, margins parallel
Lobe — any projection of a leaf, rounded or pointed

Marginal — at the edge
Marcottage — a propagation technique (*see* Chapter 4)
Meristem — region of plant tissue where cells are actively dividing, e.g. cambium layer, shoot or root tips and at nodes
Morphology — the form and structure of plants
Mucronate — ending in a short point
Mutant — form derived from sudden genetic change, which continues in subsequent generations

Node — a joint in a stalk where the leaves arise

Oblanceolate — broad end near tip, tapering toward base
Ovate — a leaf broadest near base, tapering upward

Panicle — an open and branched flower cluster
Pedicel — stalk of each flower and cluster
Peduncle — primary flower stalk
Pendant — hanging down from its support
Perianth — the calyx and corolla
Petiolate — furnished with a petiole
Petiolule — branch of a petiole
Pistil — female organ of a flower, consisting of ovary, style and stigma
Polymorphic — variable as to habit and form
Pseudanthium — false flower
Puberulent — minutely pubescent
Pubescent — downy

Raceme — elongated, simple inflorescence with stalked flowers

Recurved — bent backward or downward
Rosea — rose coloured
Ruffled — strongly waved margin
Rugose — covered with wrinkles

Scandent — climbing
Sepal — each segment of the calyx
Simple leaf — with one blade
Single flower — flower with one set of petals
Speciosa — showy, good looking
Spectabilis — spectacular, remarkable, showy
Spermatophyte — seed-bearing plant
Splendens — splendid
Stamen — pollen-bearing male organ
Stellate — star-like in form
Stigma — that part of the pistil or style which receives the pollen
Style — connecting stalk between ovary and stigma
Sub-cordate — indented slightly
Subtend — to extend under or be opposite to
Synonym — a name rejected in favour of another

Taxonomy — the name and classification of plants
Tetraploid — having four sets of chromosomes
Throat — opening of the flower tube
Tomentose — densely covered with matted wool
Triploid — having three sets of chromosomes
Truncate — as if cut off at the end
Tube — united portion of calyx or corolla

Undulate — wavy-margined

Variety — a type of modification, subordinate to species
Vegetative — growing in some way other than from seed or spore, e.g. cuttings, layers
Versicolour — variously coloured, changing colour

Watershoot — strong, succulent shoot which arises from latent buds on woody branches

Xanthophyll — yellow pigment in plants

Zygote — fertilised egg

BIBLIOGRAPHY

Anonymous. *Bougainvillea* 'Mrs Butt'. *In*: Proceedings Royal Horticultural Society, 48:46. 1923.

Bailey, L.H. *Bougainvillea. In*: Manual of Cultivated Plants. 14th printing, 1974, pp. 357-358.

Bor, N.L. & Raizada, M.M. *Nyctaginaceae. In*: Some Beautiful Indian Climbers and Shrubs, 1954. Chapt. 20, (286p), pp. 267-274.

Campbell, Killie. *The Waywardness of Bougainvilleas. In*: Gardeners in Conference. SABC, 1956.

Delap, H.A. *The Bougainvillea News*. Vol.1, 12p, 1950. Vol.2, 20p, 1951. Vol.3, 44p, 1952-53.

Everett, T.H. *Bougainvilleas. In*: The New York Bot. Gdn, III, Encyclopaedia of Horticulture. Garland Publishing Inc., New York, Vol.2, 1981, pp.472-474.

Gillis, W.T. *Bougainvilleas of Cultivation*. Baileya, Vol.20, 1976, pp.34-41.

Herklots, G. *Nyctaginaceae. In*: Flowering Tropical Climbers. Science History Publications, Dawson, 1976, pp.133-135.

Holttum, R.E. *The Cultivated Bougainvilleas I.* Horticulture. Malay Agri.-Hort. Magazine, MAHA, Vol.12 1955. pp.2-10

— *The Cultivated Bougainvilleas II. B.* X *buttiana* & its cultivars & Hybrids. Horticulture. Malay Agri.-Hort. Magazine, Vol.12(3), 1955, pp.2-ll.

— *The Cultivated Bougainvilleas III.* The Variety, *B. glabra.* Horticulture. Malay Agri.-Hort. Magazine, Vol.13(1), 1955, pp.25-36.

— *The Cultivated Bougainvilleas IV. B. spectabilis* & its Varieties. Horticulture. Malay Agri.-Hort. Magazine, Vol.13(l), 1956, pp.13-22.

— *The Cultivated Bougainvilleas V*. The Recorded Hybrids. Horticulture. Malay Agri.-Hort. Magazine, Vol.13(2), 1956, pp.66-74.

— *Bougainvillea. In*: Supplement to the Dictionary of Gardening: A Practical & Scientific Encyclopaedia of

Horticulture. P.M. Synge, *ed.*, Clarendon Press, Oxford, 1969, pp.204-205.
— *Bougainvillea. In*: Edwin Menninger's Flowering Vines of the World, An Encyclopaedia of Climbing Plants. Hearthside Press Inc., New York, 1970.

McDaniels, L.H. *A Study of Bougainvillea (Nyctaginaceae).* Baileya 21 (2), 1981, pp.77-100.

Pancho, J.V. & Bardenas, E.A. *Bougainvilleas in the Phillipines.* Baileya, Vol.7, 1959, pp.91-101.

Preston, F.G. *Royal Horticultural Society of Gardening. Ed.* F.J. Chittendon, OBE., FLS., JMH. Pub. Clarendon Press, Oxford, Vol.l, A-Cocc, 1951, p.302.

Watson, Donald, & Criley, R.A. *Bougainvilleas.* Hawaiian University Co-op. Services, University of Hawaii, 1973.

Webber, H.J. *Bougainvillea. In*: The Standard Encyclopaedia of Horticulture, 1st edition. L.H. Bailey, McMillan, New York, Vol.l, 1963, pp.533-534.

Wood, P. *Bougainvillea. In*: A Comprehensive Guide to Gardening in Rhodesia (Zimbabwe). Galaxie Press, Salisbury (Harare), 184p, Vol.l, 1975, Chapt.7, pp108-114.

Approximate Metric Conversions

To convert	to	multiply by
metres (m)	feet	3.28
centimetres (cm)	inches	0.40
millimetres (mm)	inches	0.04
cubic metres (m^3)	cubic yards	1.31
litres (l)	gallons (US)	0.26
litres (l)	gallons (Imp.)	0.22
grams (g)	ounces	0.04
kilograms (kg)	pounds	2.20

INDEX